The
MIRROR
Test

The MIRROR Test

Is Your Business Really Breathing?

JEFFREY W. HAYZLETT
with JIM EBER

BUSINESS PLUS

NEW YORK   BOSTON

Business Plus
Hachette Book Group
237 Park Avenue
New York, NY 10017

www.HachetteBookGroup.com

Business Plus is an imprint of Grand Central Publishing.
The Business Plus name and logo are trademarks of Hachette Book Group, Inc.

Printed in the United States of America

First Edition: May 2010

10 9 8 7 6 5 4 3 2 1

Library of Congress Cataloging-in-Publication Data

Hayzlett, Jeffrey W.
  The mirror test : is your business really breathing? / Jeffrey W. Hayzlett, with Jim Eber.—1st ed.
    p. cm.
  ISBN 978-0-446-55982-9
  1. Management.   2. Small business—Management.   3. Business planning.
4. Success in business.   I. Eber, Jim.   II. Title.
  HD31.H3945 2010
  658.4'01—dc22
                                                          2009037859

To the tenacious and driven men and women who have succeeded in business against the odds, in spite of themselves, and to the surprise of all the people who told them success would never happen. Booyah!

Contents

Contents

The
MIRROR
Test

Introduction

Secrets and Lies

A CIA operative is sent to the outskirts of Dublin to retrieve an important piece of information from a man named Murphy—a man he has never met.

"Drive to this area," the operative is told. "You'll find Murphy at 2:00 p.m. local time sitting on a stone wall in front of a farm. Say to him, 'The sun will rise in the east and set in the west, and tomorrow will be another day.' Murphy will then give you what you need. Return here immediately—in person. Tell no one. Murphy is a closely guarded asset. This is top secret at the highest levels."

The operative leaves immediately and boards a plane for Dublin, rents a car, and drives to the appointed area at the appointed time. Sure enough, the operative sees a man sitting on a stone wall in front of a farm. The operative rolls down his window and wanting to be certain asks the man if he knows someone named Murphy.

"Well," says the man in his deep Irish accent. "That depends on which Murphy you mean. There's Murphy the butcher, Murphy the baker, Murphy the mayor...and wouldn't you know as it turns out? My name is Murphy."

The operative looks at his watch: 2:00 p.m. He looks back at Murphy on the stone wall and says, "The sun will rise in the east and set in the west, and tomorrow will be another day."

"Oh, you're looking for Murphy the spy," says the man. "He's just up the road a bit."

Psst...want to know a secret? There are no secrets. Oh, wait, you thought I had the next quick fix, flashy guarantee, and easy solution? Not in my book. Murphy the spy is just up the road. You can find the books he wrote by the curb in a box marked "free."

In this book, the ideas may be "simple" to follow, but achieving success is not necessarily quick, flashy, or easy. It comes from doing three things right: focusing on what you do, delivering the value people demand, and selling and leveraging what you have and do like crazy to grow your business. If that sounds like a secret then so be it, but there has never been a better or more important time for businesses of any size to get back to a no-nonsense approach—one that balances both common sense and innovation. Yes, I might sound like your dad, but I live in the present. I may love the power of print, but I exploit the power of social media such as Facebook, LinkedIn, Plaxo, Twitter, Digg, Flickr as well as RSS, SEO, etc. I see them as one "tool" in our business toolbox. That's how it should be. You can't expect business-as-usual approaches to work, but you also can't expect technological innovations or financial gimmicks to get you out of this mess either. After all, they're a big part of what got us into this mess in the first place. Too many people got lazy and sloppy, relying on flash and gimmicks to create the illusion of success. We all looked for an edge, but too many of us became consumed with greed—accumulating seven-figure-plus on overextended credit lines and depending on a seemingly never-ending wave of consumer spending that delivered fat and unsustainable (and often fake) profits. Promises? Value? Best practices? Gone.

And here's the kicker: We're going to do it again. Today's volatile economies have made it challenging for businesses to operate profitably. Too many of us will look at the ideas and processes laid out in the following chapters and say, "I know I should do that..." and then not do it, abandoning our principles and making the same mistakes we made before. Think of this book as sunscreen: You might dismiss that you need it, forget to apply it, or just refuse to use it—when you need it most—but if you do, you will likely get burned again.

But here's the good news: Most businesses have never had better chances to thrive. Even in good times, many still do more with less. Competition multinational? What else is new? Economics and competition have always been major concerns for most business owners. But the core truth remains: If you are willing to look at what's working and what isn't—and take the necessary steps to fix things no matter how drastic, difficult, or different—you can succeed.

Remarkable opportunities exist for any company willing to change the way it works—or change back to the way it once worked. And what happens to those who can't or won't change? They'll end up the "last dog"—the slowest animal in the herd when the lions are chasing. The luckiest ones might settle for the middle of the pack. But the view from there is like the view my wife, Tami, has from the back of our tandem bike: not pretty. At least Tami is protected. In business, being in the middle means mediocrity, not safety. Eventually those businesses will fail the basic mirror test. If they are not already dead, they will most likely die soon.

I'm offering another way. I'm offering what that first mirror test does: proof of life.

Part One

Focus

Chapter One

The First Mirror Test

Proof of Life

In life, the basic mirror test is so simple that elementary school kids learn it: *Hold a mirror near your mouth and nose*. When you exhale, the mirror fogs. The mirror test is proof of life: You're breathing; you're alive.

In business, the basic mirror test is equally simple. If you're making money and growing, you're breathing; you're alive. If you're not making money and growing, you're dead. And if you're not growing faster than your competitors (i.e., breathing comfortably), you're dying. Unfortunately, too many businesses fall into this last category and, to borrow Billy Crystal's line from *The Princess Bride*, are "mostly dead."

Sorry if I sound all gloom and doom, but zero percent growth is not surviving, it's dying—and to be honest really, really boring. If you're going to die, you might as well do it right—shoot for the moon and fail spectacularly. So, are you really alive? What stories are you telling yourself

> You'll Look Great in
> Your Coffin Too

instead of the truth—how good you look? Looking good is no measurement of health. All the latest equipment and technology, that snazzy office space or storefront, and your belief in your business are important, but not without growth. And it starts here with a complete understanding of why you are in business in the first place.

That's right, before you build the bottom line, before you deliver value and upgrade your sales and marketing, you need to go back to the beginning. You need to focus on:

- Why you are in this game at all
- How passion is no substitute for planning
- What your "118" is and why you need it

Trust me, I've been there. I learned life's mirror test in the Cub Scouts, but learning the mirror test for business was much harder and in the end earned (and cost) me much more than a merit badge.

Despite my forays into big business, I'm not some suit with a fancy education who is reverse engineering a few multibillion-dollar plans for businesses based on what I learned in classrooms and boardrooms. I am not some guru who teaches how, but has never done (or done once and now thinks he can write a "tell all"). No. I'm a jeans-and-cowboy-boots guy who sharpened his skills and developed his ideas by actually running businesses (most of them small), creating plans, and executing them on the local, national, and international level.

I know what it's like to face the mirror test. I once saw Fran Tarkenton (who became a successful entrepreneur after his Hall of Fame career with the Minnesota Vikings) speak about the ups and downs of football versus the ups and downs of business. I remember laughing in complete agreement as he told me, "You haven't experienced anything until you've laid awake late at night wondering if you're going to make the next payroll." Sound familiar? Yes, this jeans-and-cowboy-boots guy after more than two decades ended up at a *Fortune* 500 company, but I have walked miles in your business boots and still work with small businesses all over the country.

I have even failed the mirror test. Heck, anyone can have a business fail the mirror test. I just wish it had happened to anyone but me. I made some stupid mistakes and did some stupid things, but two words sum up the biggest mistake of my professional career: *pheasant farming.*

Pheasants Are for the Birds

Early in my career (but not so early that I shouldn't have known better), I thought pheasant farming was the most fabulous idea ever. After all, I loved to hunt and eat pheasants. When I took people with me, they loved it too. And when I served guests those beautiful birds, they devoured them with delight.

My passion fueled my desire and my business plan. I reached out to a bunch of friends and associates and sold them on the idea. Many of us invested all we had. We moved quickly to capitalize on the market and never questioned or even researched the lack of competition. We became consumed with the idea. We saw money everywhere. We were pioneers. We planned to set up giant outdoor pens on the prairies where the pheasants could fly and run around as if in the wild, and then we'd process the pheasants or sell them live to hunting operations. We found a farm and a recently bankrupt (should have been our first hint) slaughtering facility. We were going to sell fresh and smoked pheasants to chefs and restaurants and stores. We were going to sell them in gift baskets state- and nationwide.

I had never invested more money in anything in my life, but it was a no-brainer to me. And that's literally what it was: all passion, no brains—the pheasants *and* me.

Do you know what you get when you buy a pheasant, raise a pheasant, and try to sell a pheasant? A huge turkey! Pheasants are the dumbest birds in the world. In the wild, they are resourceful, but domesticated? These are birds that during a thunderstorm will actually group together, turn their heads to the sky, and drown themselves. Seriously. Mirror test? Hold a mirror up to a pheasant and it'll likely crap all over it. I should have taken that as a sign, because that's what our plan was too: crap. It was like taking a wagon full of money, grinding it into pellets, and feeding it to the birds.

It is fine to *want* to corner the market in something— own it top to bottom—until you realize there isn't even a market to bottom out in. The hunting operations didn't exist yet. The gift basket people had no idea what to do with pheasants. Consumers did not know how tasty and succulent the birds were. You might think about similar stories over the years like chinchilla and alpaca farms, but at least infomercials and aggressive sales pitches fueled those crazes. This was on me; my dreams of money and passion for the product carried me away. We lost everything. I had to borrow money from family and set up long-term repayment deals with the bank for years to pay off that debt.

And every time I drive down that long lonely highway on the South Dakota prairie where the farm was—something I unfortunately often have to do—I don't just want to cry. I want to drive my pickup through the building. In fact, I'm so depressed thinking about it, I can't finish this book...

> **Success Once Is Not Success**

So, what happens when you hit rock bottom like that? Well, this was not do or die, this was just die—nothing left to do but realistically look at the wreckage and honestly confront what you've done. But I have seen similar problems with businesses that were not DOA. Some businesses started out strong, grew quickly, gained volume, reevaluated their products and services effectively, and then even optimized well, but along the way (most likely at the beginning) they still became obsolete and failed. Businesses, like all things, have life cycles. Their histories are full of cyclical patterns. (I've listed a few of my favorite business books in the Appendix.) And in business, passing the basic mirror test once does not mean you will the next day, or year, or decade...

To do this, every business—from pheasant-farming bad to Apple-Computer good—must ask itself over and over the same one-word question: "Why?"

Any Direction Is a Good One, If You Don't Know Where You're Heading

Tom White, who runs the leadership training company Profoundly Simple, said it best: "Everybody should have some idea why they're doing what they are doing." So, I ask

11

you, "Why?" And don't say, "Because." That answer might get you an A in Philosophy 101, but it won't fog the mirror. Before we can focus on the mirror tests that help you grow and protect your bottom line and excel as a leader, proof of life for *any* business begins by answering the most basic "why" question: Why are you even here—why are you doing what you do? You'd be surprised how many businesses (from the owners down to the lowest tier of employees) do not know or cannot answer that question.

Try it now. Before you get to value and sales and marketing and all the things you can do to grow—before you turn to another book or webinar that gives you microsolutions for your macroproblem—answer the question. Don't say, "I know why," and move on. Really do it. Write it down. Speak it. I'm not saying it is easy, but if you can't answer the question, then you'll not only be unsatisfied with your business, your business is probably already dying in some way. And even if you know it, say it proud: Like your body or your car, a little maintenance never hurts.

> **Why Are You in Business? Answer the Question**

I'll keep asking the question in all kinds of ways until you answer:

- Why are you even here—why are you doing what you do?
- What is it that you want to do? Make money? Build huge profits? What then?
- What is the *purpose* of what you are doing? Do you want to please people? Build the best widget? Serve the best damned cup of coffee?

- What do you want to do after profitability? Expand? Be the best in the business?
- What do you seek? Are you looking for a better way of life? A better lifestyle? Well-being? Safety?
- Do your customers know the answers? Do your employees? Do you?
- Where are you going and what do you want to be when you grow up?

Okay, okay, there I go, sounding like "dad" again, but all this is essential to any business's health.

Think of these questions as a way to understand your personal conditions of satisfaction for your business. "Conditions of satisfaction" is business-speak for the criteria used to measure the outcome of a plan or project or contract. I'm just taking it back to the beginning: What are your main criteria for the direction you want to go? I developed my conditions of satisfaction PP (post-pheasant), and whether I have been running a small business in South Dakota or moving up the ranks of a global company, the business I worked on had to meet the following conditions: It had to have the ability to grow wealth, it had to allow me to grow professionally, and it had to be fun. Those have been my conditions of satisfaction for decades, and they always remind me why I'm in "it" at all.

But don't confuse fun with passion.

Passion Can Get You More Turkeys (or Pheasants) Than Gravy

I am always passionate about what I do and sell, but following your passion can cloud your business judgment.

When I press business owners to answer any of the questions I just threw at you, most of them babble something about their passion for doing XYZ. But I don't buy that as an answer—especially if they are successful.

• It is all fine and good to *think* about getting into a business because you are enamored of and passionate about the idea—and you want to be passionate about what you do—but then what?

Simply put, owning a business (big or small) is not for everyone, and riding passion alone often clouds your judgment. Even if you ignore the high failure rate for great ideas built on solid plans, most of us would prefer not to have the never-ending responsibility of a payroll, business loans, taxes, etc. Passion for the product rather than the process makes you forget this—passion can cause you to lose your focus. Someone told me they knew people who started restaurants (a business with a huge failure rate), because someone liked a dinner or recipe and said, "You should start a restaurant." And they *listened*.

> I Don't Care What You're Selling; Passion Is Not the Answer

I don't care how much someone loves your mom's secret chili recipe. That person was standing too close to the oven with the pilot light out. Get some air and think things through. You can't just hang a sign and then wonder why your business's vital signs are faint. But that's what passion can do to you. When we're too enamored of a business idea or an idea for our business, we get caught up in what we *think* that business might do. We set unreasonable expectations and we don't stay grounded. I had learned firsthand from my pheasant fiasco the problems of putting passion before the promise of success—BAR NONE. I put that in caps because that would have been the appropriate name for the business my brother-in-law briefly thought about buying when consumed by passion.

The bar was in the middle of rural South Dakota and as we drove past its crowded parking lot one Friday night, he says, "That place must make a killing." All this based on the energy of a crowded lot on the busiest night of the week. So I reviewed the overhead with him. We thought about how many people went to the bar on average and how much they spent. We estimated revenue from the hours it would be open and with little options for growth came up with the profits for the owner: $16,000 annually including salary. Breathing, but barely.

Smart business owners know they need to think through every element of their business even as they grow and change. This is why you always read stories of how the creative and technological geniuses behind successful start-ups got partners and hired CEOs to run their businesses when they were ready to leave their parents' garage. They realized they had passion and a great product but knew they could not do the accounting, managing, and selling to make it a business. All successful business owners will need to do this eventually.

But first you need to get your passion in check and think it all through as you find your direction. And when you've got your passion in check, answered the why question, and identified your conditions of satisfaction, the mirror will start to fog. So, take a deep breath. Now, pitch me.

Elevators Are Too Slow These Days—You Need a "118"

I had him. I knew it. I had been ready with my pitch and when I got him on the phone, I sold him big time. But as soon as I heard he was hooked, I stopped. I didn't try to close the sale then and there. Instead, I tried to better position myself to take advantage of his interest and asked him for a bit of time a few days later.

"Well…"

"Let me ask you, are you an early morning person or an afternoon person?"

"Morning."

"Great, so are you a coffee or tea man or do you like juice or water?"

"Coffee."

"Milk or cream? Light or dark?"

"Milk, light."

"Bagels, donuts, muffins, or cottage cheese?"

"Bagels."

"Great. So I'll see you Tuesday morning at 7:15. I'll bring bagels and coffee and give you a fifteen-minute presentation of my product as you eat your breakfast."

Once again, my "118" had succeeded. Now, I could close the sale the way I like: in person.

The 118 is my version of what some people still call "the elevator pitch"—an out-of-date name for the worthy idea that you need to sell what

What's Your "118"?

your company offers (and you) in the span of an elevator ride. Problem is that time used to mean up to three to five minutes. Now, it's mere seconds. Technology has not only made things (including elevators) move faster but also has increased the need for speed and immediate relevance in pitching. You have seconds before I tune you out and maybe two minutes after that to completely sell me with your initial pitch.

The *118* comes from the 118 seconds you actually have to pitch: 8 seconds to hook me and up to 110 seconds to drive it home—less than two minutes with only seconds to spare. The first eight seconds is the length of time the average human can concentrate on something and not lose some focus. It is also the length of time of one of the toughest rides in the world: a qualified ride in professional bull riding. In these first eight seconds, you must be compelling, strong, and focused to be successful. You must hold on as one of the meanest, toughest animals in the world tries to throw you off—just like any good prospect will. Make it those 8 seconds, and I'll give you 110 more to drive your message home with no bull. But if you have not sold me at the end of the 118, I will start to tune out. At that point, we are moving forward to a sale or not.

I speak at hundreds of meetings, conferences, and events worldwide every year, and I am constantly amazed by the inability of entrepreneurs, business owners, their managers, or their sales and marketing representatives to deliver a great, relevant 118.

The 118, like the elevator pitch before it, sells much more than a business's products or services and unique selling proposition (USP). It is an essential piece in building your brand. It conveys who you are, the assurance your business offers, and the promises you will deliver on. Think you have a brand? Brand is the biggest business buzzword, but what does it mean? To me a brand is just a promise made and kept to a customer. Your 118 helps define what promises your brand will build or make. It connects every promise you make to those around you. Too many businesses don't focus on these promises and eventually they not only fail to build a brand, they just fail.

The 118 connects directly to the foundation of every business's growth. I'm not saying a bad one means certain failure, but I have rarely seen a good one deployed in the right way fail to help a business grow. How could it not? It conveys to anyone what he or she will get from your business.

This is usually where people start to nod their heads as if to say, "I know." But I am not looking for an "Amen." I'm looking for action. This is proof of life, people, and no time to nod in agreement or say, "I know I should do that" or "I'll get back to that after I keep reading." Even when business owners can answer the "Why?" questions (and thus know why they are doing what they are doing), the typical stammering and yammering when I ask for their pitches indicates to me a huge inability to convey what they are doing to their team and customers.

So, put the book down and write down your 118. Even if you have a good one, do it. I'll wait...Need help? I asked a few top performers about the best and worst pitches they received. Here is what a few had to say:

- "I was riding up the Gherkin elevator with Will Harris, the marketing director at Nokia. I asked, 'What if you could get dozens of user-generated videos for less than $1,000 each with www.mofilm.com?' He signed up before we reached the top floor and then Nokia went on to win the Cannes UGC competition with one of those videos." — Jeffrey Merrihue, CEO, Accenture Marketing Sciences (London)

- "This [insert idea here] gives us competitive advantage (the only factor that leads to profitable growth), and trades on the four things we covet: our core essence (what we know how to do and what our consumers consider our credentials/leverage), speed (because speed kills), surprise (because surprise disorients even smart competitors), and concentration (the only way smaller guys break through enemy lines with 'fewer resources')." — Russ Klein, President, Global Marketing, Strategy, and Innovation, Burger King Corporation

- "The worst elevator pitch is one I hear frequently. It goes like this: Prospect: 'What is it that you do?' Salesperson: 'I represent XYZ Company.' Stop! What does that do to help build the relationship we all need in sales? Describe not whom you represent but what you do to help people solve the problems they have. Why not answer with, 'I help people solve the problems of living too long, becoming disabled, or dying too soon.'" — Robert D. Lowrey, Managing Partner, Northwestern Mutual

- "The Best: We make print clickable. The Worst: We do anything and everything a company needs us to do as cheaply as possible." — Andy and Julie Plata, Co-CEOs, OutputLinks, Inc., Graphic Communications World

The next step is to know your pitch cold — you have to do more than make your own Kool-Aid; you need to drink it too. With so many pitches coming from so many media, compromising attention spans and taking up bandwidth, I have no patience for poor pitching.

> ## If You Can't Stand Pitching You, Then Why Would Anyone Else?

Work on your 118 again and again. Find a real mirror for this part of the test and talk to yourself. I do—I trained myself in front of a mirror to speak in sound bites for the media and 118s for my business. If no mirror is around, I sit in my office and speak to an empty chair.

Once you do that, branch out and try your 118 on other people. Not in front of your family (your family will lie to you and tell you you're good) but colleagues and friends you can trust to listen but don't love you so much that they will be afraid to hurt your feelings if they think it sucks. Develop friendships with other business owners and create a sort of mini board of directors for your company that can help you with these mirror test issues—not a real board for legal and finance issues, but one that can help you get back to best practices, force you to ask the hard questions about your business, and dissect your 118 over lunch or coffee.

Next, try your 118 out on your team. Then, sit in your chair, turn the proverbial tables, and listen to your employees do it to you. In fact, invest time to get everyone in your business to know your 118 too—starting with you and then working your way down to the lowest tier of employees (the part-timers, the delivery people). And not just so everyone can repeat it like they've been hypnotized but say it like they mean it and feel it! "Practice, practice, practice" is not about memorization; it is about *believing* in what you are selling so the people you pitch feel it too and sell it well everywhere they go. (We'll cover more on this and leading your employees in the next chapter.)

I always ask my salespeople to sell me before they sell anyone else, and I lead by example. I make them listen in on and take a few sales calls to the company so they can hear how the pitches are made and received and how ours compares. Sometimes I tell them that I want them to leave it on my voice mail and then I pick up the phone instead. Inevitably they get flustered but why? You should be ready with your sales pitch at any time, in any format. If I picked up the phone and then told them to e-mail me, I'd expect the e-mail in minutes too.

• Want to know if your team has your 118 down? Call them. Have someone you know make an inquiry to your company and listen in and hear how they pitch and respond before letting them free in the business "wild."

And don't limit yourself or your team to pitching in the office if that's not where the pitches will be made. You need to know your audience *and* your environment. If the pitch is on-site, find time to sit in the room you'll be using and practice the pitch there. If it is off-site, see if you can get in the room or at least understand its setup before you arrive. Think of yourself and your team as athletes on the day of a big game or race. All athletes go on the field before the game and visualize winning. You need to feel the same thing. You need to be comfortable so you can be as natural as possible.

And as Sandy Koufax, one of baseball's greatest pitchers, once said of his craft: "You get the work done by

Weight and Leverage, Not Force

leverage and weight rather than force." These words should be the foundation for any pitching you do: weight and leverage.

Weight

The last recession wiped out any chance of an easy "yes" based on the lure of easy money and plans that have nothing behind the smoke and mirrors—our mirror test's evil twin. Koufax's words remind us that presentation style is important but not without substance. (Remember: You'll look good in your coffin too, but you're dead.) You need something that appeals directly to the practical (and even emotional) needs of the person you are pitching. Energy, clarity, and style are important, but in pitching, content is king. People may hate hucksters like the late Billy Mays, but every product he pitched from car scratch fixes to cleansers grabbed your attention—he knew how to balance his debatable style with clear content that appealed to the audience's needs and sold them.

Leverage

Koufax won far more than he lost by honing his craft, studying hitters, and knowing their tendencies. He knew what the people facing him liked and disliked and could handle almost any situation. That's leverage in pitching. Leverage in business starts the same way. Knowing your pitch is one thing, but knowing your audience is another. Making every pitch as targeted as possible and understanding how what you do fits into what your customer needs informs the substance of almost every chapter in this book, but here it relates to the most primary focus of the first mirror test: making sure your 118 connects to both your business and your audience so you can make the sale and grow.

Truth is, most salespeople don't take the time to rehearse the pitch, let alone the customer they are pitching. It's not like there aren't resources to help you. Harvey Mackay's "Mackay 66" is a list of 66 excellent fundamental questions that will help you learn the intimate details of any relationship and that every person selling something should ask. (Download it for free at: *www.harveymackay.com/pdfs/mackay66.pdf*.) Yet people still fill my Facebook page, voice mail, e-mail inboxes, and my literal desktop with stupid pitches and silly messages. This is called losing before you begin. I get salespeople pitching my *Fortune* 500 company by telling me how their products are going to increase our sales by $10,000 and more—I lost more than $10,000 just reading one of their pitches. Here's a hint: I see no value in getting to know you or your family. If you get me, I'm going to ask you these pointed questions:

- What specific sales expectations do you have?
- How is your product or service going to achieve those expectations?
- What does your value proposition mean to my business and me?

If you have the answers (and the rare pitcher who does wins my respect), I will listen. If not, I will invite you to come back when you do to see if you can offer me any value. I will tell you that 99 percent never come back.

That's because even if they have a good pitch, they have no idea how to pitch to their audience. They keep hitting me with generalities instead of addressing their experience in my industry and their USP. And I'll keep pushing them, but with every wave of withering questions the calls and e-mails start to trail off. There's an old joke from the speaker's circuit about a store: Johnson's Taxidermy & Veterinary Clinic—one way or another you'll get your dog back. It could be everything to everybody; you can't.

But even then, as Winston Churchill said, "They say that nobody is perfect. Then they tell you practice makes perfect. I wish they'd make up their minds." Even great pitches can fall short for all kinds of reasons. But I'm likely to remember and even recommend to others a great pitch that I reject for the right reasons than the wrong pitch that I never should have let in the door. People who take the time to do something right—integrate my logo into the material, demonstrate an understanding of my business and revenues, show they know something about who I am—never fail to impress me. I know we live in an immediate-gratification-fast-paced-Tweeting world, but as we will see, speed without relevance is nothing.

I, like many executives (and all your customers), am more reachable than I have ever been. I am busy, sure, but the closer you get to the c-suite of any decent-sized business, the quieter it gets. It is sometimes easy to get these people on a one-to-one basis with the right approach. But that doesn't mean that we'll listen without a great 118—or buy without an equally targeted and smart follow-up.

To pass this mirror test, please don't give me long PowerPoint presentations with ridiculously cluttered and wordy slides. *Remember the Ten Commandment Rule: Like*

Moses and his tablets, get your pitch down to two slides, five bullet points each. Anything more to capture your point is too much. When you're ready, I'll listen. We've got a little ways to go yet, but I'll be here.

Bring bagels and a Diet Mountain Dew.

Just Breathe — You Still Have Work to Do

At this point, congratulations are in order: If you've gotten this far and done what I've asked, you are on your way to not simply passing but acing all the mirror tests. This first test was about taking the time to give your business a reality check and seeing if you really understand and can be clear about why you are in business in the first place. No business can fog the mirror without that.

Now, to power through on the work we've done and the promises we've made, we need to perform a mirror test for your bottom line and the three Cs that support it: community, customer, and competition. But first, we need to turn the mirror on you.

Chapter Two

The Second Mirror Test

Leadership

Okay, that's a Big Mac meal with a Diet Coke," the speaker says back to me, loudly yet still unclear for reasons technology has seemingly been unable to solve. "Please pull around to the first window."

Fast food? I've been waiting ten minutes just to order at this point. I'm hungry. I'm tired. It's cold out. And it takes another couple of minutes to reach the first window, where I pay, and the cashier asks me to pull forward to the second window to get my order. When I get to the second window, however, no food awaits me. Instead, the sixteen-year-old window worker says, "Thank you, sir. Now if you wouldn't mind, would you please pull your car up to the area on the right and we'll bring your order right out to you when it's ready."

What? I stare at the drive-thru window. "What?"

"If you could please pull ahead, someone will bring your order right over to you." I look to the right and see the designated area he is talking about where a couple of cars are waiting already: It's what I call McDonald's Purgatory.

"No, I'll wait right here."

The drive-thru window person stares at me as if I am making a joke. I'm not.

"Sir, we are really busy tonight, so if you could just…"

"No, I'll wait here." I roll up my window.

You can see the sixteen-year-old window worker has never had to deal with this situation. Flustered, he disappears, checks to see if I am still there, and disappears again. His seventeen-year-old assistant manager quickly appears. I roll down my window.

"Sir, I don't think you understand, we are really busy tonight…"

"No, I understand. I can see you're really busy. I understand it will take a couple of minutes more. I don't mind waiting. But I'm staying…right…here."

You can see the seventeen-year-old window assistant manager never had to deal with this situation either. Totally flummoxed, he disappears and now the eighteen-year-old manager appears.

"Listen," I say firmly but respectfully and before he can say a word. "This is a fast food restaurant. I paid for my food. I expect my food fast. I expect it here at this window. This is what's called an implied contract. We have a deal, but you are not honoring your end of the deal. Are you going to offer me more? Extra fries? An apple pie? No, you are telling me, in effect, to go away. But I waited my turn, paid for my service, and now I'll wait here for my order."

How long do you think it took me to get my food? As I drove away from the window, I thought about doing a sarcastic wave to the cars waiting in purgatory. But I was too busy trying to poke my straw into the lid of my drink.

*　　*　　*

The moral of this story is not that the squeaky wheel gets the grease or Jeff Hayzlett is a pain in the ass—though it does have to do with what I did and who I am. Simply put, at that drive-thru window I exhibited some fundamental qualities of a good leader: I knew what I stood for and what I wanted, acted decisively, and demanded more. And that's what you must do to pass the next mirror test: You must know what you stand for as a leader and ask for and demand more from every part of your business, starting with yourself.

In the nineteenth century, Herbert Spencer coined the phrase now commonly used in business and competitions: *survival of the fittest*. But it was Charles Darwin who popularized the phrase as a synonym for natural selection. Thus, it is appropriate that our second mirror test has its origins in Darwin. When Darwin wanted to know if an animal was self-aware, he held a mirror up to its face to see whether it could recognize its reflection as an image of itself. In similar fashion, we're going to hold a mirror up to you and see if you recognize the image of a leader.

> Do You See a Leader in the Mirror?

So, what do you see when you look in the mirror? After all, any model will tell you the mirror doesn't lie. In this case, it reveals more than the lines on your face—it reveals the lies you tell yourself in the same way. Do you look good in those leader jeans?

To pass this test, you will need to make an honest

assessment of your leadership. You will need to face the truth about yourself and your employees and start to pragmatically and unemotionally rip out, discard, shred, retire, release, and reform anything that stands in the way of success. If you can't lead, who will? Responsibility and accountability are crucial when leading a business of any size. Proof of life—the clear vision—for your business that you established with the first mirror test is impossible to maintain if a strong leader does not back it, and the next mirror test is impossible to pass without it.

- You are in charge of your own success—there's no white knight coming. Find a horse and ride.

"Ninety Percent of the Game Is Half Mental"

Yogi Berra, the legendary New York Yankees catcher, was talking about baseball when he delivered that gem of a line, but his words apply perfectly to leadership in business. In fact, having the mind-set of a leader is more important than learning tactics of leadership that fill thousands of books and seminars nationwide. After all, tactics can change and vary depending on where your business is and the type of business it is. The need for strong leadership does not. Success and growth depend on it. Your employees depend on it. The mood of your company depends on it. And this is true if your company consists of you and an assistant or even just you. Size does not matter. The millions of freelancers and consultants who make up the workforce must lead themselves.

But what freelancers know already is what every leader

eventually learns: Leadership in any business is a lonely place, because you alone are responsible for your business. Repeat after me: No one gives a damn about you.

You think the bank cares when you are late on your loan or struggling to make the next payroll? Think your customers care if they don't need you? Think your investors care if your sales plunge? Think your employees care—even those you would call the most loyal? Sure some employees care about your dream, though mostly as part of *their* dream. I'm not saying they are untrustworthy or that you should not be loyal or "go it alone." I'm saying no matter how wonderful you are to talk to, how generous you are with your time and salary, and how happy your team is, loyalty is often just a paycheck away.

I'm saying no one gives a damn about you, except you.

So the first question you need to answer to fog this mirror is not "How do you lead?" but "*Can* you lead?" Can you accept and do you want this responsibility? Be honest with yourself. Assuming the answer is "yes," stay in front of the mirror and ask these questions:

Five Essential
Leadership Questions

1. Am I acting like myself or trying to be someone else?
2. Can I read the signs in my business and be decisive and do the things every leader must do to succeed?
3. Am I the right fit for what I am doing in my business? Am I doing what I do best?
4. Am I dealing honestly with my employees and making them part of my business?
5. Can I eliminate the external (employee) and internal (ego) obstacles that hold my business and me back?

For me, these are the essential questions of leadership. Before we leap to questions about the bottom line in the next test (Do you think you can grow? Are you actually succeeding or just pretending it all looks okay? Are you rationalizing your debt question?), we need to focus on these questions starting with you...being *you*.

No Original Sin

I always say I can make a sow's ear into a silk purse—but it will still smell like a sow's ear when you open it. I can't fake it to make it, so I don't. After all, who wants counterfeit when they can have the real thing? Those people who buy fake Rolexes and bogus Louis Vuitton bags may fool some people but not all and (unless they're delusional) certainly not themselves—they will always know what they have is fake.

Copycats are even worse: They not only fool themselves about who they are and what they do but offend the people and businesses they copy. And I am not talking about stealing a process, trade secret, or system, for which there are often legal remedies. I'm talking about stealing someone's signature move, stories, or style and passing it off as your own. Think about this in your personal life: someone who always buys the same car or outfit or does the same things you do, not because you suggest it or invite them, but because that's what they do. It's probably harmless, but it is still really annoying.

We're all guilty of doing this every now and then: unconsciously or intentionally copying the best of what they know. Imitation is the highest

> **Be Original—Be You**

form of flattery, right? Wrong. Analyze other businesses' systems, think about what makes them successful, and understand the basic strategies and tactics of their leaders, but in the end, do it your own way. As a member of the National Speakers Association, I attend a lot of meetings and seminars looking for inspiration in the best and brightest speakers. Zig Ziglar, the late-great Bill Brooks, Nido Qubein, Tony Alessandra, Mark Sanborn...these are my mentors and heroes, and I use their words to motivate me. As they capture the audience with their words, I analyze what works and what does not as I think about *my own business and presentations*. Key words: *my own*.

- You must develop your own sense of style or you will lack sincerity in the words you speak and in the image you create for your business.

One time, a young man approached me after a speech and introduced himself. He told me he was a new member and starting to deliver his own speeches and asked me if he could use my "bigger than necessary" story. First, I wondered, why would he *ask* me? It's always the newbies who do this—asking for permission up front instead of begging for forgiveness when they get caught.

Then, I just wondered why. This story, like all my stories, are real-life experiences that happened to *me* in *my* business and life. Sure, it's a great story, but it's *mine*. It can never "be" someone else's, and only someone too inexperienced to offer examples from their own life would want to sell it as their own—someone not yet able to lead.

"No," I told him. "Be original."

I hope you learn something from my ideas and my

stories and find them inspiring. I want you to remember them and use them as a foundation for helping you succeed. I want you to connect them to your own experiences and then use that stuff as the examples of good leadership. I want you, if you do steal from me, to at least plug the book a few times.

But I don't want you to be me.

Some of the stuff I have done (especially in politics) is surely not for everyone. *I'm* not for everyone. I strive to create tension—you do not want to start a war with me if you cannot stomach a battle. I listen to smart people and any great idea; I care what people think. I'm just beyond caring what others think about me. When people complain to me about the content of my Tweets on Twitter, whether they are the media or my mother, I tell them to stop following me.

If you are pretending to be something you are not or caring all the time about what other people think, just stop. I want you to live this stuff yourself, not through others or me. If I want you to do anything like me, it is think like me—develop the mind-set of a leader. Businesspeople who fake it or imitate others are not thinking for themselves—they are followers, not leaders. But find your own way—it will give you faith in your decisions and how you read the signs.

Signs, Signs, Everywhere Are Signs—Read Them

I grew up on an Air Force base in South Dakota that ran, among other things, a B-52 bomber program. My dad was the senior master sergeant of the bomber program, which meant he was second in command and essentially ran the place. No one messed with my dad and that meant no one messed with me. When I went to base picnics and played volleyball, the officers stopped talking to me when they heard my name, worried about what they might say about my hard-assed dad.

One day, my dad was on call and working in our basement when a lieutenant I had never seen before knocked on our screen door. I answered before my dad did. The lieutenant told me a general inspection of the base was coming and he was going to houses all over the base to make sure everything was in order. Looking around at the toys in our yard, he suggested we clean them up and help make the base look presentable for inspection.

That's when I heard the "Thump Thump Thump" of my dad's boots on the stairs behind me. My dad was such a badass, the sound of his boots screamed authority. But the lieutenant did not realize the full impact until my dad moved me aside with an effortless swipe of his arm.

Any time I hear the word *bug-eyed*, I remember the look on this lieutenant's face as my father stepped forward, opened the screen door, and put his face inches from the lieutenant's.

"Lieutenant, is there a problem?"

"Hello, Sergeant," the now stammering lieutenant said. "This your son? Fine young man...I...no...I didn't know this was your house..."

My dad did not move or say a word as the lieutenant leaned back and looked to the right of the door to the spot where every house on the base bore a plate with the name of the occupants: Hayzlett.

The lieutenant realized at that moment he never would

have been in this situation or been forced into a frightened, apologetic retreat if he had done the one thing every leader must learn to do: *Read the signs.*

In *The Seven Habits of Highly Effective People*, Stephen Covey perfectly summed up what it means to read the signs as a leader as opposed to a manager. Say a leader decides the company's mission is to cut through a jungle with machetes. The leader climbs to the top of the highest tree, assesses the situation, and sets the direction. The leader then discusses how to proceed and what the team will need with the managers. The managers proceed to assemble, organize, and run the team (the producers), who do the cutting. Leaders then climb the tree again and keep reading the signs, looking for opportunities…and problems. In the end, the leader will be the one who realizes, "Wrong jungle!" while the manager will yell back, "Shhh, we're making progress!"

If a leader is too involved in the day-to-day activities and cannot see the forest (or jungle) for the trees, that leader will miss the signs when things go bad or, even worse, when things go "good." Fail to anticipate success in business and build on it, and you'll fail to win more and grow. Fail to balance thinking and action, and you'll never even get started.

> **Deliberate and Act—Don't Be Afraid of Ready, Fire, Aim**

So, Deliberate Carefully…

You can't jump at everything; you must consider what you want and need to do. This has helped me in every business I owned or worked in: Even if people knew I would create a stir, I would never be a bull in a china shop destroying everything for the sake of action. The people I work for and who work for me trust me to deliberate carefully.

...Then Act Deliberately and Decisively, Even If It Means a Setback...

I have stopped major announcements the night before because I felt something was still wrong. I have refunded payments for major jobs because I knew we delivered crappy results and service and I felt the loss would cost me more in the long run if I did not eat the money on the lousy job.

...And Don't Be Afraid of a Little Ready, Fire, Aim

When I left my small business life and started working for larger companies, I deliberately took each company's brand message and turned it on its head. My goal was to stretch the brand and push it to gain greater acceptance and more relevance—even if that meant causing some tension. Once I even commissioned a video that mocked my company's corporate culture. I wanted the video to shake things up—show how the future was not the past. People, including the person I replaced, told me not to air it. And I thought about it. I literally got physically ill thinking about whether or not to show it. But I did. I knew it was the right thing, and I pressed on. And the audience loved it—even the people who told me not to do it.

I do this as a leader all the time: Move the boundaries

to keep moving forward. In this case, we needed recognition for how we were changing and we were now on our way. We had taken a small but public step toward changing the way we do things and how others perceived us. I told my bosses not to worry about any more backlash. "The worst thing that happens is I say, 'My bad,' and then explain why I did it."

Now, be careful. I am not saying do as I do *or* exactly as I say here. Remember, I'm the guy who will get his hands dirty—who does the things most people can't or are unwilling to do. The point is not that I succeeded but that I pushed my company and myself to think differently. So, what are you not doing? What is the acceptable version of this approach that works for you to ensure you never get complacent about success?

We always want to know the steps we take are in the right direction, but often we can't. And then we wait way too long to act. I always say, if your plan is solid and you feel good, do it. Who is going to die? These are not life and death decisions. Most businesses can sustain a little "ready, fire, aim." If you want to test something out, go for it. As long as you are ready and it is not some quick fix solution, you'll at least learn something. Don't waste an opportunity to fire and always wait to aim. Go with your gut and don't second-guess yourself. You'll know when to press on and when to give up.

A leader who runs a great business must know how to take these kinds of risks, move quickly, *and* be smart. Leaders choose what to implement wisely and make sure what they do is working—and modify or replace it if it isn't. Even when it comes to employees. Even when it comes to customers. Even when it comes to you.

Figure Out Where You Best Fit In—and Fire Yourself from the Other Jobs

I am a sales and marketing guy. When someone asks me what I can sell, I sound like Brando in *The Wild One*: "Whaddya got?" I have sold soap, a cure for disease, printers, printing, political candidates, digital cameras...But I do not care to look at spreadsheets. Will I? Am I good at it? Sure. But I turn them over to a skilled technician. That way, I can stay focused on and leverage my extreme advantages in sales and marketing. I make sure I know what goes into and how to work every part of my business, but I cannot do it all—no leader can.

> **Leaders Must Be Honest with Themselves**

This is another one of those times when people start to nod their heads as if to say, "I know." And then they do...nothing. The reason they do nothing is that leaders are *always* doing too much. We are action-oriented people. But even action-oriented people must learn to be reflective. The mirror demands it.

• Action-oriented leaders who don't stop to reflect on what's happening often can't redefine themselves and then veer off into the weeds and lose focus.

As a business grows, leaders must be honest with themselves about who they are, where they need to improve, and where they need help. You need a board of directors? Database management? Consultants? Accountants?

Salespeople? Leaders must hire people who are smarter and better in the areas they are weak in and even where they are strong so they can do what they do best. First, decide what you do best and what deserves your focus. Then, hire people to do the rest. In other words, fire yourself from the other "jobs" that take up too much time and compromise your growth.

And remember, the mirror doesn't lie so don't try to fool it. We're talking about leveraging an advantage you have, not doing what is the most fun or difficult. *Just because you like to do something, doesn't mean that is what you do best, where you fit best, or what is best for your business.* Just because you think you are a people person, doesn't mean you should do marketing. Hey, the best waitresses are "people persons" too. Doesn't mean all waitresses are good at marketing. In fact, waitresses are best at customer service. They may never work their way to the top and may never want to get there. You're already there: Don't serve your business—lead.

Now, About Those Employees...

Google "quotes about employees" and you'll find hundreds of smart, pithy lines from corporate giants like Howard Schultz, Steve Jobs, Donald Trump...I have heard these and other leaders of the biggest and highest profile companies in the world unified in their belief in a productive, passionate, and positive workforce. These leaders did not become rich and have their companies listed among the best to work for by hiring lousy workers or failing to motivate the good ones. I neither disagree nor claim to say it any better than these people, so I won't. Nor do I want to bore you with "tips for dealing with employees" that fill countless bookshelves and websites.

| The Rules You Must Follow with Employees |

I will, however, claim to speak for and quickly deal with the things that really fog the mirror when your business is not anywhere near the *Fortune* 500, 5000, or even 50,000—the rules you must follow as a smaller business as you grow and hire people.

Six Rules to Remember

1. Ask employees…
2. Involve everyone and make it a priority.
3. Chart progress.
4. Reward good behavior, confront bad.
5. Remember: Mood is everything.
6. Fire People.

Following is a bite-size portion (or more) of what I mean by each rule.

Ask Employees…

Unless your family works with you, you spend more time with the people you work with than your family. Your relationship may be professional, but you still need to personalize your workplace to make your employees feel like they are part of the company. The best way to do this is to watch, follow, and—most importantly—engage your staff. Spend time with employees asking questions: That's how you win before you begin. Ask them questions like, "How are we doing? What can we do better? What can I do better? What's the one thing we can give our customers?" Then actually *care* about, *listen* to, and *act* on their answers.

• If you can do this, you are going to improve as a business and a leader. You're going to turn your employees into your customers' associates. They will all start working to improve your bottom line.

I have a very structured process for working with my team. I sit down with them or my managers every week and ask, "What are three to five things you did last week and what are the next three to five things you want to do? And what did you learn from what you did last week?" If that is too much for you right now, start small: Ask each employee, "What's one thing I can do for you?" When the employee answers, "Pay me more," say, "I hear ya, and we will work to do that. Thanks. Now that you've said that I'm going to come back this time next week with the same question." That's when the employee begins to think about an answer.

Involve Everyone and Make It a Priority

In all my businesses, all my employees (from the front desk to the corner office) are informed about and involved in every aspect of the business. I believe in complete transparency. In the next mirror test, I will show how you must extend this to exposing employees to your bottom line—from your pricing to your profits (something you cannot do in many big businesses)—but that starts after you make sure as a leader that everyone feels like they are involved in the big picture and contributing to the success of the business. This shouldn't be unusual, but I'm still surprised how rare it is. I know no better way to demand the solid support you expect.

• Involve employees in decisions. Bring them to meetings and help them make the right contacts. Coach them as they prepare for meetings or sales calls to ensure they're successful.

Chart Progress

As part of their involvement in the business, have your managers or employees work with you to set clear goals and follow budgets, and then work together to achieve them. Chart the progress constantly. Every week I do a one-on-one management review and discuss operations. I try to set up clear ground rules like FAST (focus, accountability, simplicity, and trust) or SOAR (superior operations, one company, align resources, replicate success) for all my employees. Do this, and progress reports are easy—everyone will already know how far they've come or fallen.

• Trust your people enough to let them make small mistakes—mistakes that won't cost you much but are of great value for them to learn from and minimize in the future.

Reward Good Behavior, Confront Bad

Enough said. Plenty of material and people are out there to give you ideas on how to do this—just remember to do it to keep your company's mood positive.

• When you confront any bad behavior that warrants a reprimand, record what the employee did and you said. Write it on a $20 bill if that's all you have and stick it in the employee's file. It will be the best money you ever spent.

Remember: Mood Is Everything

The mood of your employees reflects the mood of your company. I've seen businesses go from sky high to rock bottom on the bad attitudes of their employees and leaders. Nothing gets in the way of delivering your promises like bad attitudes. A business is a living, breathing thing made up of relationships, and like any relationship, if the people are disconnected and negative, your business will be too. Make the community of employees strong and they will sell your business—people will want in...or out!

The obvious way to do this is to come up with activities that create camaraderie like barbecues at your home or group outings and retreats. My friend at Partners & Napier hosts (on her dime) a regular Friday happy hour for anyone who shows up. The less obvious way is to make employees live up to the standards you set.

• Be fair, be diplomatic, but make sure those standards are enforced. Creating a positive attitude doesn't mean you can't be aggressive in pursuing those standards—it depends on it.

When I bought my New Horizons computer franchise, the business was not doing well. The employees were down, and it started at the top: The owner had been going through some tough times and, from my perspective, had let the place go to hell. It looked depressing. I needed to clean house and so I literally and figuratively cleaned and made everyone who worked for me participate.

We all came to work in jeans. I ordered Dumpsters, and we threw away everything. We painted. We cleaned our desks, what I called "mom on Saturday" clean. We scrubbed the grey tile in the kitchen where everyone (customers and employees) ate and discovered it was actually white. Things began to improve. Working together, the team felt they had a stake in the company on some small level.

Next, we cleaned up ourselves. I believe in the service business when a team looks good, the business looks good—it's the first step. So, I put everyone into matching shirts and asked them to wear black bottoms. Then, I enacted a zero tolerance for excuses as well as bitching and moaning. Don't just say something sucks or isn't right. That's just a bitch or a moan. Rather, if you don't like it, complain but with a suggestion for action. That's a genuine complaint—an actionable problem brought up by an employee asking for change and wanting to enact that change.

My first chance to enforce my standards with the employees came when the shirts arrived. When a manager moaned that he should not be forced to wear a branded shirt like a "common worker," I gave him a choice: Take the shirt or leave the job. He stayed and became one of my most important managers. He must have sensed my final rule to remember.

Fire People

John Stewart, a rabble-rousing consulting star in printing circles well-known for turning around businesses, told me that to get over any fear in running my business and to stand behind my convictions as a leader, I should fire the first person I saw when I got back from his seminar. "If you see John, fire John." Well, after the first few seminars that year, the team soon caught on, and on the morning of my return to the office, they would say to the new person, "Jeff will be back from the seminar soon. He likes a Diet Mountain Dew when he walks in the door. It would be good if you gave it to him." If no one new was around, everyone spent the morning avoiding the entrances lest my axe fall on them.

Ridiculous, right? Of course it is. It never happened. But it is no more ridiculous than *keeping* everyone you hire. You know there's differentiation among your employees. Who isn't delivering on your promise and furthering your goals? Draw a line and make the tough choice to weed out the bottom tier and bring in new people to upgrade your team continuously. Don't get too comfortable and settle for what you have: This is what unemployment insurance is for. If you have charted progress and given feedback, if you have been fair and given them the tools to succeed, no one should be surprised, let alone you. Can't think of a name? Ask your top performers; they will give you a name.

- "I love you, I'm going to miss you, move on"—Breaking up should not be hard to do in business. You must be willing and ready to fire employees including freelancers (and as we will see in the next chapter, even customers).

Get rid of the people who suck up your time without delivering equally dramatic results. Get rid of every person who believes his or her rules are more important than yours. Get rid of the analog people who cling to the same-old ways and dated systems so you can bring in new people who see new ways for the digital age. And get rid of that part of you that will always bring you down.

Busting Johnny Vegas

I've built and sold several successful businesses following the six rules I just mentioned. There's nothing like watching a business you love thrive and grow, and then, for me, selling it for a profit. I remember one day soon after I had sold a business for a huge profit, I was strutting around the house thinking about my next opportunity, and my wife seemed to be really upset with me.

I asked what was wrong, and she said nothing. So, I did what any husband would do: I waited a couple days and hoped it would go away.

But it didn't, so I asked again, and she asked, "Do I really want to know?" So, I did what any husband would do: I said, "Yes," even though I had no idea what she was talking about. But I was feeling pretty darn good about myself; I could take whatever she said.

"Ever since you sold the business," she said, her voice filling with disgust. "Every time you speak, you just act and sound like you think you're God."

Well, I heaved out my chest, looked down at her, and pointing my finger I spoketh unto her and...I got the point. But she was wrong about one thing: I wasn't God at that moment. I was Johnny Vegas. I was suffering from one of the worst afflictions that can strike a leader: Johnny Vegas Syndrome.

> *Johnny Vegas Syndrome* (noun)
>   1. A crippling business disorder that strikes leaders of any sex, race, ethnicity, or size usually following a great success or triumph or sale, etc. Characterized by an exaggerated swagger, metaphorical swinging of chains, and Rat Pack screen savers. Symptoms include unbearably inflated sense of self and an undignified belief that you are bigger than yourself and the community that surrounds you.

Johnny Vegas Syndrome is only the most exaggerated of the myriad internal obstacles leaders must avoid from a lack of sincerity to failing to trust others to talking too much to getting consumed by anger to relying on the same-old-same-old instead of exploring new opportunities. But Johnny Vegas is the worst. I have seen too many successful businesspeople like me suffer and lose control from its condition. It is the evil outgrowth of success. Even in its mild form, it brings down the mood of the business and offends customers and everyone around you. It leads to bad decisions that can destroy a business's bottom line by making you think nothing can touch you. The only known cure is failure or a metaphorical slap in the face from someone you trust.

There are plenty of mistakes business owners make that will cost your bottom line short term more than these internal obstacles, such as making assumptions about what's on the customer's mind (instead of taking notes and capturing data), not giving the customers what they say they want (winning an argument but losing the sale), and the biggest sales blunder of all: failing to ask for the order. But these mistakes affect your bottom line not your ability to lead.

If you can bust Johnny Vegas and deal with internal obstacles, continue to take responsibility and be accountable, and follow the rules to remember when dealing with employees, you have almost passed the second mirror test. All you need to do is get lost.

Okay, Leader, Take a Break and Pass This Test!

I know it's hard. If you love what you do, it should be tough to walk away. But the mood of a business depends on leaders leading by leaving. I would be a lousy leader—not to mention parent, friend, and boss—if I couldn't let go and leave for a day, a week, even two without things falling apart. Show faith in your systems and employees and go recharge to maintain balance in your life.

That is the operative word: *balance*—between your

work, family, personal (friends and hobbies), and spiritual lives. *Work* is just a word in that equation—only one of four—but we forget that. To remind my employees and myself of this balance, I give all the people who do a good job for me a handmade Lakota (Sioux) Indian medicine wheel. A small circle divided into four equal parts with each part painted a different color, the wheel is about harmony between the colors, seasons, elements, directions, and the balance we all need in life.

After all, no one will make you stop working so hard. When you're an alcoholic and people know it, they stop giving you drinks. When you're a workaholic and people know it, they give you more work. They pat you on the back and say, "Good job!" If you're the leader of a business, you've probably not only done this to the people who work for you but you've done this to yourself.

> **You Must Have Balance: Give Yourself a Break**

We've all been there. I used to pride myself on being the guy who never took a break, no matter how much I deserved or needed one. For three years, I never took a vacation. Period. I was so far down that road, so addicted to my work and consumed with that Johnny Vegas I-can-handle-it mentality, that when I finally reached my breaking point I did not take a vacation…I checked into rehab—a three-week program in California for all kinds of addicts. Not some spa for white-collar burnouts—people struggling with drug and alcohol and other addictions surrounded me. But I was going to break my habit.

And then it happened. As I'm sitting there in the crowded seminars, speakers delivering their motivational talks, my personal notebook of materials on my lap, I can't help myself. I start running numbers: How much did I pay to be here? I look at the room—packed: How much did they pay? I look at the speakers as they come up and think how much their fees and expenses run. I analyze my notebook of materials they gave me—what's the printing cost here? And I start figuring out the spread. Numbers filled the pages in front of me. Even when I added in the property costs, I knew they made a killing. So here I am in rehab for being a workaholic, and I'm thinking how to get into this business?

Crazy? Not quite. I don't want to minimize the seriousness of being a workaholic as a business owner. I made it through that rehab session, and while I still inevitably struggle with my balance, I always remember it needs to be there and I find it. But I am also me. I always say, "If you want to be like me, seek medical attention." But what I could add here is: "If you want to be like me, seek medical attention. Rehab profits are enormous." I always look for an angle in the world around me, and I need to be true to that side of myself as well.

So, like the McDonald's story that opened this chapter, the point of my rehab story isn't just what it appears. What I was doing in my seminar was exactly what you must do in your business every step of the way: Run the numbers and understand the bottom line and how to grow it. This is the stuff of our final mirror test.

The first mirror test forced us to know what we are doing and why we are in business. The second compelled us to take the steps necessary to be responsible and accountable to our business, our employees, and ourselves. Now, assuming you have taken that break and found your balance, we are ready to perform the mirror test for the bottom line and the three Cs that support it: community, customer, and competition.

Chapter Three

The Third Mirror Test

The Bottom Line

A soldier joins a platoon on the front lines, eager to serve. "Tell me what to do and I'll do it," the soldier says to his commanding officer. He is immediately assigned to guard the perimeter.

"Sir," the soldier says. "I'm on it. All I ask you is that you get me a gun."

"Son, I don't have a gun," the CO says as he looks at the ground. "But here's a stick."

The soldier takes the stick and stares at it. "Um, permission to speak freely, sir? It's a stick."

"Son, I know it's a stick. But I want you to carry this stick at your side. If the enemy attacks, I want you to point that stick straight at them and go, 'Bangety, bangety, bangety. Bangety, bangety, bangety.' They'll drop like flies. And if they get past your fire and it gets to hand-to-hand combat, use it like a bayonet and go, 'Stickety, stickety, stickety. Stickety, stickety, stickety.' And they'll drop there and then."

The soldier is not sure what to make of this. He stares at the stick but does not question his CO further. He starts to patrol the grounds, hoping the enemy does not attack. But sure enough, early that morning while he patrols the far edge of the perimeter, the enemy attacks. By the hundreds, they advance over the hills on the camp. The soldier yells and radios for help but it is too late. All alone, with no time left to doubt, he takes a deep breath and points the stick.

"Bangety, bangety, bangety." To his amazement, the enemy soldiers start to fall. He keeps firing, "Bangety, bangety, bangety. Bangety, bangety, bangety." One enemy group manages to avoid the soldier's fire until they are upon him. This time, without hesitation, he thrusts the stick forward like a bayonet. "Stickety, stickety, stickety. Stickety, stickety, stickety," he yells as he lunges at his attackers.

Soon, all around the soldier, there is nothing but fallen bodies. The soldier is feeling pretty good about his stick. Then, over the hill comes one more enemy soldier.

"Bangety, bangety, bangety," yells the soldier confidently. But the enemy soldier keeps advancing through every shot and is soon upon the soldier.

"Stickety, stickety, stickety," yells the soldier. But the soldier and his stick just bounce off the enemy onto the ground.

As the enemy walks over him, the soldier feels his bones being crushed. Lying there in the mud, his stick snapped against his broken body, the last words our soldier hears are the enemy soldier saying...

"Tankety, tankety, tankety. Tankety, tankety, tankety."

The most important message for small businesses and this final mirror test is not "get a tank" but "*think* and *act* like a tank"—know what your weapons are and how to compete with them. Know your targets and know your tools. Most business owners don't and will never have all the tools to deal with everything on their own—so don't pretend to or you'll end up like our soldier. Sure, you might think you need a tank or at least an antitank weapon *right now*, but if all you've got is a peashooter don't waste your time building or buying a bigger weapon—exploit what you have and build the best peashooter, win the fights you can win first, and then level your competition.

Bigger-is-better tank-like approaches are almost always fueled by greed and turn out to be unrealistic, unworkable, and sooner or later destroy a business. You want to think big enough but not bigger than you are. Stop spending more to generate less. Stop expanding before you're succeeding, decreasing profit percentages as the business grows. Stop thinking a new flashier website or a bigger media campaign or a nicer office is the answer to all your problems. Better to make what you have right now better than anyone else's and build that bottom line with an eye on profit (instead of revenue)—that's what keeps your business fogging the mirror.

In the first mirror test, we applied this "better-is-better" approach to your conditions of satisfaction. In the second mirror test, we applied it to you as a leader. In this third and final mirror test, we continue this systematic rethinking

Better Is Better

of your business—taking everything apart, throwing out what does not work, building up what's good to grow the bottom line, and dealing smartly with your community, customers, and competition.

The inspiration for this final mirror test is one we

all know: *Snow White*. "Mirror, mirror on the wall," the Queen says. "Who's the fairest of them all?" Just as in this book, the mirror does not lie: The Queen is not the fairest; her competition, Snow White, is. So, the Queen acts with all her might to destroy her.

But in the end, the Queen fails. Snow White does not pretend to be something she is not. She is more likable (with a happier soundtrack), has a more loyal community (those dwarves and forest friends work hard for her), and the ultimate customer (Prince Charming) sees the most value in her. Snow White may not have been bulletproof (or appleproof) to the competition's attacks; she barely fogs the mirror at one point. But because of her advantages, she not only survives, she wins.

So, are you the fairest of them all? Think one poison apple, one "Tankety" Queen, can't bring you down? Okay, enough with the fairy tales: Think you are connected to your community, know your best customers, and can best the competition? Well, the answers won't matter—and you won't pass this last mirror test—unless you understand these two things first:

- Buzz is *not* sales.
- *Never* compete on price.

To help you remember this, repeat after me, "Whoopee cushions and file cabinets."

A Whoopee Cushion Makes Noise Too

"And we know this campaign is going to create fantastic buzz for the product."

The presentation from my team up to this point had

been pretty good. They believed in the plan they pitched. I had been ready to hit them with the same hard questions I ask anyone pitching me, starting with "What specific sales expectations do you have?" But that question was now effectively, as lawyers say, "Asked and answered."

There were no sales expectations, just the usual bull about buzz.

And so with images of drowning pheasants racing through my head, I did what I always do when people talk to me about buzz: I told them to buzz their way right out the door.

Without specific sales expectations attached, buzz is like a whoopee cushion: a joke that has all the noise and none of the consequences of the real thing. Yet far too many people

> **Buzz Is Not Sales**

in sales and marketing (in-house or out) talk about *buzz* as if it is a synonym for sales.

But buzz is *not* sales. Sales are about revenues and profits. The goal is to sell something for the greatest return you can get, and good sales are defined as a customer's cash in your pocket and both parties knowing it was a good trade.

Remember: If you have identified a market for what you're trying to sell and a critical mass of people in that market who want what you have to offer, anything you do to sell to them must have specific sales expectations. Perhaps buzz is useful for a business like a nightclub to generate word of mouth, a big opening, and brand it the "in" place. But what happens when the buzz goes bye-bye? There better be a plan in place for generating sales.

In trying to keep up with our multichannel, multimessage

ways of doing business, don't get sold on whiz-bang technologies or Google analytics or offbeat marketing and ad campaigns and promises of viral videos in a vain attempt to attract customers solely with flash. Don't listen to people who throw around terms like *brain campaign*. What does this mean exactly? Does any business *need* a brain campaign? Well, maybe those who get into the pheasant farming business. No, wait, that's a brain transplant. Anyway...

Truth is, buzz is usually just a way of talking without selling. Maybe that's something big businesses can afford. You can't—and you can't afford to compete on price either.

The Four File Cabinets of the Apocalypse

When I owned my print shop in Sioux Falls, we loved when lawyers came after us: We did a lot of business for the top law firms that needed a substantial amount of copying done for their litigating lawyers. When I heard news of a big case about to start, I would contact the firms involved and offer our services—all they needed for ten to fifteen cents a copy, knowing they marked up those copies to twenty-five cents for their clients. I wish I could have found a way to put more of that 10 cent markup in my pocket, but my price was fair and I made decent profit of 20 to 30 percent on even the big jobs, which ran $1,500 to $2,000—a lot in those days (and I still think a lot today for one job in any small business).

But one day I found a way to make 70 percent on one of the biggest jobs we ever had without lifting a finger except for dialing a phone number...*of my competitor.*

It started when one of the law firms we solicited called us with a big request.

"Hey Jeff, we've got a job for you but it's big."

"Okay, how big?"

"Stockbroker-case big. Lots of evidence. Four file cabinets' worth of material."

You know those old cartoons when characters see the chance to make it rich and dollar signs form in their eyes? This was a $4,000 job! I quoted them my usual price per copy, a ten-day turnaround, and arranged to have the local moving company pick up the cabinets immediately and deliver them to us for $50. Now, I am always a proponent of outsourcing specific services that you do not or cannot provide. (When you have a heart problem, you see a cardiologist not a primary care physician.) But at this point, I had no idea I was about to outsource more than pickup and delivery.

When the file cabinets arrived, my dedicated and loyal staff looked at the full-size extra-deep four-drawer cabinets bulging with folders stuffed with stapled documents and odd-sized sheets and nearly staged a coup: "Oh my God, Jeff…holy…are you crazy? This is a disaster. It will take forever." But all I'm thinking is dollar signs—dollar signs!

Then, one member of my team says, "Jeff, isn't our competition running that three-cent-copy promotion?"

"Are they?" I say, immediately remembering why I love my employees, especially when they listen. The dollar signs started to morph into something better: dollar signs with my big cowboy boot attached to kick some you-know-what. We dialed our competition.

"Hi, are you still running that three-cent deal?"

"Sure," says the voice on the other end.

"Okay, well, what if I have a lot of copies? I mean really a lot a lot."

"Well, what's a lot?" says the voice.

"Four file cabinets' worth."

"Oh, no problem we'd love to do that!" the voice replies.

"I really need this quickly, very quickly, too."

"Sure, we can do it in two business days," says the voice delighted to be closing the deal.

"We'll be right over!"

I call the moving and storage company and tell the truck to turn around. The cabinets were probably in my offices for less than an hour before they were on their way to the competition. An hour ago, I saw dollar signs for a $4,000 job, which would have cost me in time and labor about $2,800. Now I was getting it done on the same machines in less than half the time for $1,200, more than doubling my profit—and my client got the job faster. Of course, my competition paid the price, literally. In their haste to finish the job, they made a mistake and deducted 20 percent of the total.

All this proved the point my employees had learned from me: If you compete on price, someone like me—a customer or a competitor—is going to clean your clock. Someone (again, like me) with the time, knowledge, and money is going to take advantage of you and it will keep happening. Forget what anyone has told you, with the exception of grocery stores, I am 99.9 percent sure this is

> **Never, Ever Compete on Price—Ever!**

right: The single biggest blunder you make as a business is competing on price.

- Look in the mirror and repeat after me: Never develop a reputation for having the lowest price or fee and never sell or compete on price.

I ain't too proud to beg: *Please, please, please, stop being the one who charges less.* I am not talking about pricing fairly or package pricing (buy five, get one free) with still substantial built-in profits over and above your "nut" (cost of doing business). I am talking baseline one-to-one product or service sales that undercut your competition or try to "compete" with big business. Leave the pricing game and loss leaders to discounters and big-box retailers who make fewer customized products and write off the losses as "marketing." Did you know those big-name high-end luxury brands write off their ridiculous rents on New York City's Madison Avenue as marketing? There are things you can do with a large business that you just cannot do with 2, 20, 200, or even 2,000 employees. Price "whoring" is a game you do not want to get into, a game you will lose — to them or to people like me.

My competitor did, and I knew it. He and I used the same machines, and this was the kind of print job I knew I could not do for much less than eight cents a copy if I wanted to make a profit. My competitor was doing it for three cents, so there was no way he was thinking about profit — he was thinking about volume as a way to build his business. But if you are losing money on sales, you can't make it up on volume. Plus, I knew how many machines he had and to do my job in two days would virtually tie them up. Where do you think those people who needed small jobs fast would come during that time?

This is why I cringe when I hear someone say, "I can do it cheaper." What makes you say such a thing? You see a sale slipping away and the voice in your head starts discounting. ("Hey, the price is $2,500, but I could give it to you for $1,500." "You say they can do it for $500? I can do it for $300.") Think you can just hang a sign offering huge deals and start a little price war? You will ruin the marketplace for any business. Plus, your customers will keep asking for bigger discounts and expecting more for less. And before you know it, you are just like all the pond scum that starts underpricing and destroying the market for nothing.

Instead, I want you to start charging *more*. (No, that is not a typo.)

I don't care what kind of economy we are in: I would rather charge for everything and make money and deliver on all my promises than take a job to lose money and compete on price. Small business customers do not come to small businesses because they offer the lowest price. They come to them because of one word: *value*.

Small businesses are about customization, service, and attention. They are about individual customers (people or businesses), and we must build our business around those relationships. Trust me, if your customers perceive your product or service as low quality and offering little value to them, they will leave, regardless of price. This is why Apple—big company that it is—can charge a premium for all its products: Its customers still feel a personal connection and believe in the quality and value of the product.

The only way to fog this final mirror on an ongoing

basis is to stand and sell. Not with fine-print tricks that add unexpected costs ($100 for a window...uninstalled): Be clear about what it is you're offering and set and meet the highest standards for selling it.

And never, ever give it away.

If you get stuck with budget problems from your customer, anticipate the concerns and work with them—but do not charge less for what you are doing. Listen to the objection and be empathetic like my friend Robert D. Lowrey at Northwestern Mutual, who starts by saying, "I was thinking of your concern about your budget. Let me show you how this solution fits into your budget." And then do what my friends Andy and Julie Plata at Output-Links, Inc., do and propose an immediate solution for the problem that is between $X and $Y that would allow the deal to close but adjusts *both* deliverables and costs.

After all, profit trumps everything, and selling you or what you do profitably is the only way to survive. Without it, you've got nothing.

Today, When I See a Pheasant, I Shoot First

When I lived and worked full-time in Sioux Falls, I used to meet regularly with a group of business owners—a sort of mini board of directors. We had started meeting years before when I was in the printing business and all of us had $1 million or more in sales. Our group met regularly around town and attracted a guy who knew our names and businesses and longed for a seat at our table. One night, he offered to buy me a drink and as we waited, he told me, "I've got only $750,000 in revenues, but I can't wait to be in the $1 million club."

Now, this was no kid out of college. By most measurements, this guy was a decent businessman. And yet he had no idea how to think from the profit perspective.

"Buddy," I said, "You do not want to be in that club. You want to be in the $1 million *net* club. You want to be in the 20 percent profit club, the 40 percent profit club. Develop a profit goal—not a gross sales target, a profit goal. Revenues are not a measure of growth or success or I couldn't buy *you* a drink." I paid the waitress.

In my experience, businesses profit from profits. Do you have a different experience? My primary condition of satisfaction for getting involved in a business is the ability to grow wealth, which to me means a way to grow profits (not just revenues) successfully. This is what I call the profit perspective, and it is built on one simple belief: Profit is good. Not greed, profit. I know this sounds pretty basic, but too often we measure success on revenues alone.

If you feel guilty about making a profit, then you are doing something wrong. *Profit* is not a dirty word. It is actually a three-letter word: *net*, and a part of every business ledger. Profit gives us the lifestyles we want and allows us to provide for others and ourselves. Thinking about how you run that profitable business has to be second nature to you, or the mirror will slowly stop fogging.

- Decide what you want from your business (a better lifestyle? flexible hours? time off?).
- Figure out what you need to charge to achieve that lifestyle (x dollars to make x percent profit from my sales).
- Build that amount into every product and service in your profit center.

Your profit center consists of the products, services, or activities that make you the most money. What are they? Find them. Learn how to mea-

Find Your Profit Center

sure them—make sure you treat time as an inventory and add that into the costs—and figure out at what point you make money from them. Then, continuously devote your time and energy to those types of services or products or activities—selling the heck out of them to secure your present and your future by servicing them well and creating new services around them.

Having this profit perspective will help you survive the leaner times and thrive in better times. But watch out for Johnny Vegas. Let him lead you not into temptation during flush times. Johnny Vegas *loves* to overexpand. He sees all that cash on hand and makes you believe you can never outgrow yourself. He'll make you believe that size matters—that twice your location equals twice your money and twice your customers. And he'll make you think you need to act *now*.

When I owned my print shop, we had a thriving downtown location that provided 90 percent of my sales. I had another location I bought that made the other 10 percent. Whatever it made and fed to my downtown business, I realize now I suffered from a mild case of Johnny Vegas Syndrome and moved too quickly without running the numbers.

The simplest way to avoid this is to remember the old line: You get what you measure. Know what your metrics are for monitoring and measuring so you can make decisions based on real information. Learn how to evaluate and keep evaluating return on investment (ROI). Formulate a budget with net and gross targets. (Countless books, classes, and websites help you do this in depth. Find one that speaks to you or is recommended by someone you trust whose company is making a good profit.)

To keep myself focused, I like to keep a piece of paper with information that is most important to my business in front of me at all times. I call it a "dashboard." At my *Fortune* 500 company, that can get fairly complex, covering everything for a project from the executive summary to the media pool to sell-through and sales activity. But for your business it could just focus on daily and weekly gross and net sales to keep the proper profit perspective.

And nothing helps boost those profits more than doing the right things with your three Cs: community, customers, and competition.

Community

For years, I've joked about why I was an usher in my local church. I'd tell people I wasn't just an usher because I wanted to be closer to God; I wanted people to see me, to see me active in my community, and to raise my profile with the members of that community...and for them to get used to me taking their money.

The point is no matter where I am I know my business is visible through me. And if I were ever shameless enough to put a brochure on a collection plate, I would still be completely 100 percent upfront about what I was doing. Remember: Leaders are not deceptive or deceitful about who they are or their involvement in a cause. I am devoted to my communities, but I see nothing wrong with giving back for other reasons too. I've been in politics as well as business, and I never play the game of the worst politicians: I tell you what I think, not what you want to hear; I tell everyone in all my communities what I want—your business—and what I can do for you.

There are countless ways to involve and get involved in your external communities to the benefit of your business. Join and host political campaigns and professional organizations. Participate in fund-raising drives. Sponsor events. Work with civic groups like chambers of commerce and other local business groups. You don't need me to tell you what to do or how to do it; you just need to make sure what you do makes you happy and delivers value to your business. And then use social media to stay connected.

More on all of that later. But for the sake of this final mirror test and your bottom line, there is one community we often fail to involve and inform on every level, and it is the one we spend more time with than any other: our employees. If my primary condition of satisfaction for getting involved in a business is the ability to grow wealth, I need everyone in the shop knowing what this means and how we get there.

> **Make Your Business as Transparent as Possible**

• Open your books to your team to help everyone focus on profitable sales. Put your trust in them to work with you to achieve your goals. (And if you can't trust the ones you have to do this, fire them and find some you can trust.)

Some may disagree with some of my employee tactics. But this one...this one I take flak for all the time. I hear, "They'll steal from me" or "They'll tell people how I do business" or "They don't understand." But don't you think they *already* understand on some level? Don't you think they know when you buy a brand new Mercedes and your kids are in private school and there is energy in the business and you're smiling (*really* smiling) that things might be going well? And don't you think they know when someone is let go, orders come in COD, and cash is scarce that things are not?

I want my team to know from the start how things are and how we charge and where they fit in. I call this my "Z-Out Mentality." The Z-Out was a key on my printing business's computerized cash register that gave me my total sales for the day. I have no idea why it was

My Z-Out Mentality

called Z-Out, but I knew when I hit it I would know where things stood not just for the day but the week, the month, and the year—and so would my team, which is why we all gathered together to Z-Out. Since I had already plotted what I needed for my daily, weekly, monthly, and yearly totals and shared that too, we all knew what the numbers meant, what the history was, and where the day fit in the averages we needed to reach my growth goal (10 percent).

The Z-Out Mentality means your team is working together to meet and exceed sales targets—and has a stake in your success.

- They work and sell as a team and see your business as a whole, not simply an unrelated series of individual sales, customers, products, or services.

- They not only work in a culture of managing budgets and understanding how to achieve budgeted results but feel accountability for staying within those budgets and achieving those budgeted results.
- They know what to expect in the big sales months and which months are usually in the toilet (oh, how I hated July) so they can maintain perspective and know what was normally good or bad.
- They know how to evaluate opportunities in this context too—if things are bad, a great deal from one of our suppliers might compromise our cash flow, but in a good time could boost our profits.
- They even dress better lifting the mood of the business.

The Z-Out Mentality can also help control your labor costs by connecting your labor intimately to your costs. Labor is the most expensive and intensive part of most businesses—you may love to be around people, but they're expensive during the day and go home at night. Z-Out allows you as a business owner to know what you need in terms of getting rid of those people who are a drag on your bottom line and what you need at the top as you search for potential rainmakers to bring in—two things you should do constantly. In the meantime, with everyone focused on the bottom line and sharing your profit perspective, everyone shares responsibility for growing his or her piece of the proverbial pie, improving your ability to prospect and close new business, building stronger customer ties, and facilitating team selling to the best customers.

In the end, the Z-Out Mentality is about connecting

your dreams as closely as possible to your employees. Loyalty may be only a paycheck away, but if your employees are connected to your dreams they will work harder and will understand how to connect and deliver on your customers' dreams as well.

Customers

More pie, no gravy-sucking pigs…more pie, no gravy-sucking pigs…One fall day this became an essential mantra of mine.

On this brilliant fall day I was in Bob's office waiting in the outer area to go to lunch with him. You know the kind of day I'm talking about: cloudless and pleasantly cool, the smell of leaves in the air. Everything about the weather just brightened my already good mood. Business was good. Profits were up. And I was having lunch with a great friend and customer who was…running late.

Now, I hate waiting, but Bob and I were close not only professionally but also personally. He was one of my printing company's biggest customers and we saw each other regularly outside of work too. We enjoyed each other's company and shared the same interests, especially golf; while playing we would have long conversations about business and life and nothing at all. We even liked each other's wives and children. For Bob, I'd wait.

So, I sat in a chair and looked over at the sales materials Bob kept on the waiting area table. (Bob's smart like me: No magazines for him—he'd never miss an opportunity to sell!) That's when I saw it.

Until that moment, I thought I was intimately familiar with every one of Bob's sales materials. After all, I printed them. But the one on the top was unfamiliar. I picked it up and I did what all printing people do: I looked at it from all angles, I felt it, I smelled it, I tasted it…and I confirmed what I knew the second I saw it: We did not do that job. That it was of a quality I was not sure I could match in-house did not matter. What mattered was I had not had the opportunity to try. When Bob emerged a few seconds later, apologizing for being late, he knew immediately from my face something was on my mind, and I told him.

"Hey man, I saw this on your table. Nice. Why didn't you send us this business?"

And Bob said, "I didn't know you did it."

Failing to make the offer and ask for the sale is a sure-fire way to leave money on the table. Your grandmother probably said it best: You don't ask, you don't get. But this was worse. I could not even make the offer, because I had not put my business in the position to make the offer to one of my closest friends and most important customers—I had taken my relationship with Bob for granted. To this day, if I stumble across the Bill Murray/Richard Dreyfuss movie *What About Bob?* on cable I nearly vomit.

| The Three Customer "Nevers" |

Regardless of how close you *think* you are with your best customers, every day you must be in their faces, because even the closest ones are not thinking about you. Only you are. Time for me to pound more "nevers" from that lesson into your brain:

- Never take a client/customer for granted.
- Never assume you really know your customers.
- Never stop selling your company to your customers.

In a hypercompetitive, global business environment, what you do tomorrow is what matters to your customers, not what you've done for them lately. Loyalties are fleeting so we need to consistently and fiercely connect in the right way: the way that matters to the customer. Relationships in business must focus forward!

Ask your best customers questions like, "What does my business mean to you and your business? Why do you come to me? What are you planning and how can I fit in? Where are your biggest needs? What are your dreams?" My feeling is no one is completely satisfied so ask those customers what you can do better for them. Find out what they want from you and what is most beneficial to them—what makes them happy? (Creativity? Helpfulness? On-time delivery? Persistence? They can go anywhere for a better price, but they can't go anywhere to be happy.)

Then, just like you did with your employees, actually *listen* to the answers. Working with your customers is 10 percent talking (presenting and pitching) and 90 percent listening—stop listening to the sound of your own voice and listen to what your customers have to say. Pay attention to even the smallest details.

Not sure who your best customers are? Just remember Pareto's Principle, also known as the law of the vital few or most commonly the "80-20 Rule," which states that 80 percent of your business comes from 20 percent of your clients. This is as true a rule as I have ever encountered, particularly in small business, which is why so many business books continue to cite it. For the purposes of this book, let me say this: *If you don't know who your 20 percent is, then you're not even close to fogging the mirror.*

You're already dead because you don't know what's most valuable to you.

I like to call my 20 percent "pie" and the 80 percent "ice cream." The pie is the substantial and filling part of the dessert; it supports the ice cream, which fills in the spaces. Bob was part of my pie and I blew it. Maybe I let our friendship cloud my business judgment, but no excuses, I failed. After our lunch, I drove back to the store more determined than ever to know everything about my pie people. Just like I did with my employees, I resolved to upgrade my customers—to make and keep new customers and maintain our current relationships at the same time and then use that knowledge to attract 1, 5, 10, or 20 more like them.

As I drove past my store and the huge plate-glass window that made up most of the front, I could clearly see the only person who could have made my day worse than it already was: Thelma.

Gravy-Sucking Pigs (noun)
1. Customers, vendors, or employees who suck up everything at the "trough" of your business—far more than their fair share—and are still never satisfied. Usually allowed to feed much longer than they should and must be put to slaughter as soon as possible. (See also, Thelma)

Calling Thelma a "gravy-sucking pig" has absolutely nothing to do with her physically or as a human being. I loved Thelma dearly. She was a matriarch of my hometown. In some ways, she was like a second mother to me, helping with introductions to important people or giving me tickets to concerts she sponsored. She was also my biggest customer from hell. Whenever my staff saw Thelma approaching through our big front window, they raced to the back, leaving the last one in front to deal with her. That explained why all but one of my team members were hiding by the back door when I walked in.

"Thelma," they said together quietly.

"I know," I said.

"She hates it again," they said.

"I figured," I replied, listening through the door as Thelma told the counterperson exactly what was wrong this time, something about the blue not being the blue she wanted when she changed it from the blue she picked before.

"But we did everything exactly as she asked," they pleaded.

"I know we did. I did the job this time."

But that didn't matter. No matter how many times we proofed, how many times we checked the job, or if it matched the deliverables exactly, it was still *wrong*. It didn't even matter if it was not our fault. A package she ordered got stuck in the snow in Gainesville, Georgia, for four days. *Gainesville, Georgia!* It snows in Gainesville, Georgia, for a day every other year. This storm was the lead on all the national news, and she blamed...us.

Despite our close friendship, we lost money on every job we did for Thelma, and that's a game I could not play for anyone.

So, I fired her.

I did the easy part first: I grabbed her file and called one of my competitors. This time I told my competitor exactly who I was. I explained who Thelma was, her order history, and her problems. You see, your customers from hell can be your competitor's dream-come-true and benefit both your bottom lines (as was the case with one of my competitor's customers from hell he sent to me a few months later). My competitor agreed to take her on. I sent her file over with one of my employees.

Now came the hard part. Unlike underperforming employees or vendors who don't deliver what they promised, gravy-sucking pigs often have an endearing quality to them that make them hard to confront (think *Charlotte's Web* only without the web). But I knew I had to do it. I called Thelma into the store.

"We got a problem, Thelma."

"Dear, what is wrong? Are you in trouble? Do you need money? Can I help?"

"No, no," I said. "Listen, I love you dearly. You are wonderful to me and I know you want to do so much for us. We love that you want to be our customer. But we can't do the kind of quality you need. We can't live up to your expectations. So I made arrangements with this other business to take you on. I think you will be happier with them and they can do a better job for you."

Thelma took it as well as she could despite the shock of my words, and you know what? My competitor did do a better job because she let them—something she only did because I let her go. I turned her away and all the Thelmas that did not make me money and focused in on my Bobs.

• More pie, no gravy-sucking pigs...that's what fogs the mirror and keeps you strong when facing the competition.

Competition

Some people that have known me for a while might be surprised that this section is so short. For a guy who used to speak about "ripping the head off the competition," you might think I mellowed. For a guy who stomached the business of political war rooms and gathered all the dirt he could by almost any means necessary to damage the competition, you might think I'm holding back. But if you've done everything in this chapter, you are already far less vulnerable to the competition than you think. You just need to compete smartly.

You now know what your weapons are and how to compete with them. Now, you just need to know your targets.

Remember the inspiration for this final mirror test is Snow White. She was more likable, had a more loyal community, and made her prince happy. The only thing she lacked to make herself appleproof was awareness: She had no idea who the Queen really was. You must. Yet I'm always surprised when businesses do not take the competition seriously and research the competition clearly. I think many businesses would have just as much luck asking a "Magic 8 Ball" about their competition based on the information they have. Will my competition beat me today? "All signs point to yes."

Sometimes I hear a business owner say, "I don't worry about the competition." That's nice. As Mark Twain said, "Let us be thankful for the fools. But for them the rest of us could not

> **Who Are Your Competitors? Do You Know Them?**

succeed." I often jokingly say that if a company doesn't have an enemy it should get one, get to know them, and race as fast as possible to get ahead of them.

But first answer one basic question:

• Who are your competitors? Other small businesses? Franchises? Big businesses like big-box retailers and chains?

The greatest weapon you can have to prepare for and deal with aggressive competition is information. Know everything about these competitors. What did they make or lose last year? Who works for them? Who is on their boards or advises them? Whom do they contribute to in the community? What alliances do they have? Who are their biggest customers? What kind of technology do they use?

Now, quantify and qualify this competition. Do a SWOT (Strengths, Weaknesses, Opportunities, and Threats) analysis of each one and evaluate your position against them:

- How much business is at stake?
- How do you compare?
- How can you get ahead?
- How can you build on your strengths and capitalize on their weaknesses?

And finally, go back to our first C (community) and use the competition to build it. Sometimes the best people are working for someone else—find out why and start forming a plan to get them. See who works at those businesses you admire and engage them. Get to know them at industry and social events. Search for the rainmakers and have those people help you—not the competition.

If you can do that, the next time you face your competition—breathing, with a strong sense of focus, a complete understanding of your conditions of satisfaction, ready to lead, and sporting a sturdy bottom line—they'll need more than a poison apple to knock you out.

Because you'll be thinking, "Tankety, tankety, tankety."

Testing 1, 2, 3...Did You Pass?

Congratulations, your three mirror tests are complete. It's time to build on your focus and understand your value to maintain your success. But before we go there, look in the mirror one more time and ask, "Do I like what I see? Do I like who I am, what I stand for? What do I stand for?" As your business grows and goes through all the ups and downs that each cycle brings, your core values—what I call your personal value proposition—will get tested time and again.

When one of my businesses failed (not the pheasant farm—a *real* business), I was devastated, but I was most disappointed that I could not

> **What's Your Personal Value Proposition?**

immediately do right by the people who trusted me to succeed. These vendors and other businesses had extended my business credit, which I could not now repay; most of them would get a quarter or less on the dollar I owed them after the deal I worked out with the bank.

But after they were paid their percentage, I called each one of the small businesses I owed. I told them that I knew I did not have to and I did not know how long it would take me, but I was going to pay them back in full.

One of the people I owed was my lawyer (who only got $1,000 of the $6,000 I owed him), and he told me, "Jeff, listen, this stuff happens in business. I can't speak for everyone, but what's done is done. I'm writing off the loss."

But I wasn't done.

For a few years, as I built my new businesses successfully, I did everything to collect receivables on that now defunct business. I became my own personal collections agency. I went into customers' offices and when they pleaded poverty, I took whatever they had. "You're using that old phone system? I'll take it. What's in there? Magnets? Ship those to my storage facility."

Three years later, I sent my lawyer a $5,000 check, and he called me very confused.

"Jeff, I...what is this check?"

"It's the money I owe you from three years ago."

"Are you crazy? You don't owe me anything. The bank reduced that debt. I wrote it off. I don't even have any invoice or receivable to credit it against."

"Are you saying you don't want the money? I mean if you are rolling in so much cash that you can't take a little more to go on a vacation or buy something nice for you and your family, I think I feel a lawyer joke coming on."

"No, no, I...thank you. You didn't have to do this for me."

"I am happy to do it. You're welcome. And I didn't do it just for you...I did it for me." I then did the same thing with every one of the businesses on my list. Well, all except one, whose owner was really mean to me—that money I spent on her competition.

I wanted my lawyer and all the people who trusted me

to feel good about me again so I could feel good about me. This was how I decided to take responsibility for my mistakes and hold myself accountable. This was what I felt was the right thing. ·

This is how I was able to look myself in the mirror. I'm not saying follow my lead. I'm saying it's up to you to determine how you face yourself in the mirror and honor your personal value proposition. There are shortcuts for a lot of things in business but not this.

Part Two

Value

Chapter Four

The Liver and Onions Principle

Winning Before You Begin

The Youth Business Academy was ready to roll. The intensive one-week summer program, run by the South Dakota Chamber of Commerce and held at my alma mater, Augustana College (a small Lutheran school in Sioux Falls), would bring a few hundred of the state's best and brightest high school juniors and seniors to campus to teach them about free enterprise. The students would meet business leaders, set up mock companies, sell products, compete with other students' companies, and so on. Enrollment was high and offered a terrific opportunity for the college to market itself to top potential students from across the state.

My job that summer was to run the hospitality program and help Augustana impress the high school students. And as a twenty-one-year-old college senior, I knew if we were going to impress them, we needed to feed them the food they were going to eat when they got to college. I told Augustana to stuff them silly with cheeseburgers, hot dogs, French fries, pizza, and milk shakes.

"Sugar them up and set them loose," I said. "When it comes time to fill out college applications, they'll remember they ate great at Augustana."

"Got it," said my supervisor. "It will be handled."

Of course, I believed it would be done. I did not ask how or when or who would do it (he did not say he would). I did not know or think that I should. I did not think about it as I ran through my checklist on opening day. It never crossed my mind as I strolled through campus to the first event, tipping my cap and nodding hello to a group of senior-citizen women who strolled past me on campus.

No, my college did not double as an assisted living facility. As the Youth Academy was scheduled to start, Augustana was finishing an adult learning program during which 300 older women took classes in archeology, the history of Norway, and the Great Depression. Not a problem. Think nothing of it. The seniors and teens wouldn't interact at all except...in the cafeteria. *Problem*.

There was only one cafeteria on campus, and for the seniors' last day, the food service people had prepared them a special meal of their choice: liver and onions. Is there a less hospitable meal for high schoolers? What was worse, it was the only item on the menu.

I'd like to tell you next about how I raced across campus to dining services and, finding steaming trays of liver and onions, fired up the grills and personally cooked hot dogs and whipped up milk shakes for 300 students—the king of hospitality! I'd like to tell you that, but like I said, I never thought about it until it happened. That night, it was liver and onions for 600—seniors *and* students.

The Liver and Onions Principle

No matter what we fed the students the rest of the week, they couldn't recover from the horror. It didn't matter how much fun they had or what they learned, whom they met or how great the campus was. It was all liver and onions. They told their friends about the liver and onions. *Their friends told their friends about the liver and onions.* The tale grew bigger each time until my beloved alma mater had become a stinking gossip mill of liver and onions.

Seriously, it took a few years for Augustana to recover. If this had been the age of texting and YouTube, we might still be doing damage control. Instead of capitalizing on a great opportunity, we lost enrollment from bad word of mouth—all because no one confirmed what was on the menu that first night and I assumed it had been handled.

Success is simple: Losers lose, and it's better to win. But nothing is worse than losing with success in sight, especially when you could and should have known better. As much as I like to go for it, I have conditioned myself with three words to avoid failure by jumping too quickly into the doing and selling. Before I launch any business plan or initiative, I think *liver and onions.*

• Whether you have a multimillion-dollar company, a shoestring start-up, or any-sized company in between, attempts at breathing life into your business will fail if you do not constantly determine, ask, and answer the right questions—and make sure those answers are implemented.

But what are the right questions, and how do you ask them? Well, you're already on your way! The three mirror tests focused on many of the essential questions you needed to ask about understanding why you are in business in the first place, confronting yourself as a leader, and dealing with your bottom line. In the next three chapters we will concentrate on questions and assumptions surrounding value—how you deliver and get it—to keep the promises you make to yourself, your business, and your customers and sell to them.

You must...Wait, did you just nod dismissively at what I said thinking I would mistake it for an "Amen!"? Don't worry; I see it in my audiences all the time. "Jeff, this is so obvious!" the nodding heads indicate. "We always ask questions first." Nah, you shoot first. Trust me, I'm a hunter. I know a thing or two about shooting, and most people are an easy target in this regard. I'd tell you to look in the mirror and ask yourself the question about questions, but instead, turn to your partner or spouse or best friend or even a customer and ask them, "Do I ask questions or talk first?" Actually, if you're like most businesspeople, you won't say it like that. You'll pose a rhetorical question or say, "I ask questions, right?" If you time it just right, you'll catch the people you ask rolling their eyes before trying to find a nice way to say, "No."

> You Don't Know What You Don't Know

The point isn't just asking questions but getting past your assumptions of what you know, learning the *right* questions to ask, asking them, and then listening to the answers. In this social-media-dominated Wiki-centric world in which we are encouraged to comment without thinking and talking at people is mistaken for talking with people:

- Stop assuming you know it all.
- Stop downloading comments before you ask the questions and hear the answers—and then thinking those answers are being implemented.
- Stop and ask for the sale and then evaluate where you stand.

Remember, in talking with customers, 90 percent is getting information (listening); 10 percent is giving information (presenting). My *What About Bob?* problem centered on failing to ask one of my biggest clients what he needed. That's losing before you begin. That's "liver and onions."

Losing Before You Begin: Making Assumptions

If you've seen me on *Celebrity Apprentice*, at the Oscars, or on the floor of a trade show, you know I clean up well. But when I'm home in my natural habitat, outdoors on my horses, dressed down doesn't begin to describe me. I'm wearing faded jeans, a comfortable work shirt, a jacket I can get dirty, and scuffed up cowboy boots I never polish. When I'm not riding Blaze or another one of my horses, I get around in a beat-up pickup truck, its sides dented and streaked from mud and dust, its windshield pockmarked from unpaved roads.

I was in town running some errands in this pickup when I suddenly thought, "I want a nice leather desk blotter for my office." And over the course of the next hour, I couldn't shake the idea that I had to have this thing. I may be a social media devotee, but I'm still a pen-on-paper, note-taking guy. (How do you think I stay awake in all those meetings and calls?) I wanted something nice to take those notes on. It wasn't rational; I simply knew I wanted a really nice one for my desk. It would make my office complete.

I also knew this was not the kind of item you purchase in a big-box retailer. This was an ideal small business purchase—practical but fueled by a personal desire for something special and high quality, not mass-produced and low-priced. So I drove to a local office supply/stationery store and walked right past the counter to the area with the desk accessories. I was pleased: The choices were great, a few different sizes, options, and prices. I started thumbing the leather of one of them.

The sales associate followed me, though he clearly wasn't interested in my business. He had eyed my wardrobe, my truck through the window, and my boots (that even though I wiped on the mat probably still had bits of Blaze on them) and made an assumption about who I was and what I wanted. At that moment, I knew exactly how Julia Roberts' character in *Pretty Woman* felt when she walked into that fancy Beverly Hills clothing store dressed in her "night" clothes: judged by my looks and dismissed based on impressions drawn from that little bit of information. I never figured it could happen to me *in my hometown.*

Go Ahead, Judge a Book by Its Cover but Never *Ever* Judge a Sale by One

"Sir, can I help you?" the associate said, his stiff greeting the only question he asked.

"You sure can," I said, ignoring his tone. "Tell me about this pad."

"Oh sir, I'm afraid that's very expensive."

"I didn't ask how much it cost. I asked you to tell me about it—how is it made? How does it hold up?"

"Well, like I said, it is very expensive. They are all very expensive. I'm not sure you realize that."

I wanted to say, "Are you kidding me? I'm not sure you realize you lost this sale. Then again, you didn't go in expecting to *make* a sale, did you?" Actually, what I wanted to do was stand on one of the sample desks, point down at him, and utter my favorite line from Shakespeare's *Julius Caesar*—a line I use in business all the time: "Cry 'Havoc,' and let slip the dogs of war that this foul deed shall smell above the earth with carrion men, groaning for burial." Then, I would flick a piece of Blaze from my shoes in his direction and storm out. But instead, I said thanks and walked out without another word and without a purchase.

• Being in business is always going to be a battle, but better to battle the competition than your customers and yourself by thinking you know it all.

You can remember all the advice and questions from my mirror tests. You can know why you are in business and have your pitch down. You can hone your leadership skills and train your team. You can know what you are selling, to whom you are selling it, and how you will sell it to them. You can cover every aspect of the three Cs. And you can still be done in by your know-it-all assumptions.

The simplest way to avoid this in business is to remember a common PR formula, "Always win the RACE."

RACE

R (Research: Define the program, know the facts, set objectives, define audiences).

A (Action: Plan the program).

C (Communicate that action and execute the program).

E (Evaluate the results).

The next two sections deal with the ACE part, but quite frankly, most people lose before they begin the R phase. In fact, I have seen some incredibly detailed programs fall apart simply because I or someone else in the room asked some very basic R questions like, "Do we have enough money to move ahead and enough capital to sustain it?" or "Are our expectations reasonable given these objectives?"

Preparation in the R phase also extends to making sure your team and you understand the objectives you have set so everyone can pursue them relentlessly. That's why we spent so much time making sure your community of employees has a stake in your success and believes in themselves, the company, and the product. In the R phase, the team should extend that stake by practicing pitches and testing messages like they are doing a reading of an early draft of a play—hearing how it sounds in front of a loyal but critical audience of colleagues and friends to know what to expect and address any obvious problems before spending money on its production.

But R really comes down to asking the hardest questions, considering different perspectives, and preparing for withering assaults both fair and unfair. As you consider the value your business or any initiative your business is launching offers, imagine being audited by the IRS or interrogated by an unrelenting detective. What question would bother you the most if asked by one of them? Now, answer it. What if you saw that question in a newspaper or in a blog post? There are people out there who want nothing more than to take your skin off.

When I did *Celebrity Apprentice*, people said I had a "face for radio" and asked if my wife wanted a recommendation for a personal trainer for me—nothing about the content of what I said. You need to remain thick-skinned and unemotional, and ignore them—even more so when confronted directly.

Asking and answering the hardest questions is often called tackling the elephants in the room—the big points and important topics that are often missed and left unsaid and unaddressed. Maybe because we live in a micro world where the word *elephant* takes up more than 5 percent of your 140 characters, but 140 characters is plenty to ask the question, "What am I not seeing?" In business, we miss the elephants all the time. There is an elephant joke that stems from the assassination of President Kennedy and the subsequent shooting of Lee Harvey Oswald in the Dallas police station by Jack Ruby that sums it up perfectly: "What did the Dallas chief of police say when the elephant walked into the police station? Nothing, he didn't notice."

Lives are not lost when we miss our elephants, but we will lose something by not talking about them. In thinking about this more, I went back to my Rolodex (yeah, I've been at this a while…I still call the thousands of contacts in my BlackBerry my Rolodex). I asked a few executives and business owners about the hardest questions they ask and answer as they prepare to launch a major initiative (and that they now ask themselves every time):

- "What are your partners' objectives? This applies to distributors, advertisers, investors, licensees, anyone you're doing business with. Too often people assume there's not just an alignment but a consistency of perspective on wants, needs, risk tolerance, metrics for success, goals, etc." — Christie Hefner, Former Chairman/CEO, Playboy Enterprises, Inc. (the longest serving female CEO of a public company)

- "I ask five questions: Where are we going? How will we get there? What's in it for me? What's expected of me? Where do I go for help?" — Keith Nickoloff, President, Pharos Systems

- "What is the goal of this initiative, how will it improve profitability, and how will you measure your success six months from now?" — Paul R. Edwards, President, Form-Store Incorporated

- "I often refer to the saying that there are two really important aspects of life. One is to get a good meal, and most of us get that. The other is to get a good night's sleep, and few do. So, after you've exhausted yourself and your team preparing for that major campaign or pitch, ask yourself the question, 'Will I get a good night's sleep?' This is an acid test that digs deep into your core. Sure the numbers look good, the ideas are great, but all too often we ignore that gut feeling we get when we're afraid to take one more look…Try it; you never know, you may wake up with the answer to any question that may be asked." — John Williams, President, Mud Worldwide

All of these responses reminded me of the hardest question I ever asked myself in business. I was launching a partnership with a friend. Our plan was solid and we were ready to move on to the ACE phase when I kept feeling the lingering presence of an elephant. When I figured out what it was, I called my partner into my office and asked him, "What happens if one of us dies? How are we protected? How are our families cared for?"

I had realized our partnership was so deeply connected to each other and the loss of one of us could derail the whole business if something unexpected happened. And while neither of us wanted to imagine this worst-case scenario, we had to for the good of the business and ourselves. So, we decided to take out insurance on each other. If one of us died, the other would get the money he needed to buy the surviving family out of the business, and we made our wishes clear to our families.

• You may not know what is going to happen, but you can prepare for what you know *might* happen.

In business, and I would say most times in life, that's the essential first step in winning before you begin. Here then are my questions to get you past that first step successfully.

Win Before You Begin: My ACE Questions

There is an expression craftsmen use, "Measure twice, cut once." Most businesses confuse measure with measurement (as in return on investment). They rarely take enough time to truly measure what they know with questions. Whether I work for a multibillion-dollar company, a shoestring start-up, or anything in between, these are the questions I always ask and take the time to answer when I am about to launch a big initiative, product, service, store, etc., to understand my intrinsic value and reduce the risk of ever having to kick myself and say, "Why didn't we think of that?"

My Top Twenty Questions

The Questions You Must Ask Before You Start

1. What are you selling?

Go back to Chapter 1 and figure it out.

2. How much business/money is at stake?

Is it worth it? What are the revenue and profit goals? Quantify and qualify.

3. Is the process repeatable/scalable?

Does it have enough and can it add enough zeroes?

4. What have you done to assure you can pull this off?

Do you have the cash/capital, people, and systems in place to do what it takes to succeed? Treat time as inventory and ask how much you will need.

5. To whom are you selling?

Identify your customers—from age to sex to race to education to relationship status…anything that will help you "know them" personally and help them feel a personal attachment to you/your business and your product/service.

6. Are you selling to those customers in the right way?

What is your positioning strategy and its components? Are you promoting the right product with the right message at the right time? Loyalties are fleeting, so consistently and fiercely assure you are connecting in the right way.

7. Are you charging what you should charge?

Charge what you are worth—do not compete on price!

8. Are you focused on quality?

Your value proposition is not connected to price.

9. Can your target customers afford what you're selling?

Your value proposition is moot if your customers cannot fit it into their budgets.

10. What and how much analysis have you done to come to the conclusions and answer the questions asked so far?

Now is not the time to assume anything or rely on your gut.

11. What is your unique selling proposition (USP)?

What sets you apart or makes you stand out? What makes you a better or more reputable or valuable business to the customer?

12. What is your customers' connection to this USP and what you are selling?

Value is an emotional connection—you need to satisfy a need or want with what you sell. What is it? The big boys know theirs. Think McDonald's just sells low prices with their value meals? No, they sell comfort. They sell "Happy Meals." How do you help a customer achieve this level of feeling?

13. How do you compare to the competition in terms of what you are selling?

How and why are you different? Read about them—all the information you can get and not just the information that you agree with. Talk to former and current clients about them. See the job they are doing. Shop them. Call them up. Stalk them. Follow them. See how they react.

14. What will the competition do and say when you begin?

How will they respond? Anticipate: What would you do if they launched something like this? Have five scenarios prepped and know what to do if each one came up. What if they cut prices or offer a free service or attack you—how will you respond?

15. What will your customers and potential customers do or say when you begin?

You need to know what can happen when you take your value proposition to the public. What will their behavior be and how can you capture it to your advantage? Do you expect immediate reaction and sales, or a slow build? Will they understand immediately or need it sold to them over time? Look at past projects to help you understand.

16. What will your team do or say when you begin?

Do you have the right team to represent you in the right way? Do they believe in what you are selling and how you are selling it? A body is nothing without a brain—you must look and sound like you know what you are doing.

17. Have you given that team the tools they need to succeed?

They should be prepared and prepped to sell. Some of this is covered in the R phase. Make sure you do it again now with all the materials and paperwork in place.

18. What could go wrong and how have you prepared for that?

Don't just prepare for the worst—play out the entire disaster on paper and see if there is any way to prevent the problems from ever happening by making small adjustments to your plan in terms of timing, scale, target, etc.

19. How will you measure your success?

Remember: You get what you measure.

20. When will the needle start moving?

Patience may be a virtue, but you'll drive yourself crazy waiting if you don't have a sense of timing.

I developed these questions, because like so many business-people, I've been the bull in the china shop; I just went and did it and I did not think or care what was in my way or what I knocked over. But ironically, even though I always ask these questions today, people *still* think of me as a bull (as opposed to just full of bull)—they think I'm not asking them. Part of the reason they think this is my confidence and belief in everything I do and sell. But most of the reason is that I can answer these questions faster the thousandth time through. The more you ask the better you get, and the better chance you have to cream the competition.

• Even my split-second decisions are based on experience and preparation. In other words, I always measure twice and cut once; I just do it quicker than you.

Truth is, if I didn't ask these questions I could never face myself in the mirror. I need to make sure I am doing what I am doing the right way every time—not just the fastest way even if it is something I've done a thousand times before. Why do you think even the best doctors use a marker to identify the right leg, kidney, or other body part they need to operate on? There is no shame in being thoroughly responsible and accountable, maximizing your chance of success and minimizing your risk of failure every single time.

Losing After You Begin: Failing to Make the Offer

Recently, Tami and I were watching TV one night when an infomercial for a new elliptical bike came on. I was immediately sucked in. It looked like something I would use and certainly need—those Five Guys cheeseburgers are hard to resist! Tami would be so proud of me for taking the initiative to get in shape.

"Hon, we have *got* to get one of those," I said proudly.

But instead of eliciting a loving embrace, Tami's head spun around like Linda Blair in *The Exorcist* and she screamed, "What?"

"I gotta get one. Look how great it is!" I said, thinking she must have thought I said *she* needed to get one. But the look on her face indicated otherwise.

"You have got to be kidding me?" she said, hoping I was. "Are you serious?"

I wasn't sure what the problem was so I kept going, repeating the "facts" about the benefits of the bike from the infomercial and how aerobic activity will help me get in shape.

Finally, she couldn't take it any more. "Are you crazy? What are you talking about? What do you throw your clothes on every day in the bedroom? Go look." And in the bedroom under my shirts and jackets and suits from the last week was the elliptical bike we had purchased less than a year ago for me to get in shape.

The answer to the question was right in front of me and I missed it. I had forgotten. Unfortunately, too many businesses make the same mistake: Forgetting the obvious—asking for the sale. Just like no one can look in the mirror for you, you are responsible as a leader to ensure that you and everyone who works for you always make the offer.

> **You Cannot Lead If You Don't Ask for the Sale**

If after all those questions, you don't ask, you will never get.

Please, please do not have this problem. The most blatant mistake businesspeople make—and a surefire guarantee their businesses will stop fogging the mirror—is failing to ask for the sale. Why does this happen?

- They get caught up in the pitch and fail to close the sale.
- They assume that the offer is implied.
- They are afraid to ask.
- They don't know how to ask.

Do us all a favor, whatever the reason, if you can't make the offer: Get out. You can't be in business if you can't ask for the sale. You cannot lead. You cannot build revenue and profits. You will never get the chance to do more than talk about your value to your customers, and talk in this regard is truly cheap. In fact, it's free, because with no sale, no money ever changes hands.

Winning After You Begin: Reflect and Begin Again

Not all talk is cheap, however. I believe you learn continuously in business, and talking about your experiences, reflecting on them, and evaluating them is the final step in winning before you begin.

Wait—did I just say you win before you begin after you have ended? Absolutely.

Preparation for success the next time comes in reflection and understanding how well you delivered the last time. No matter how fast the speed of business today,

The Liver and Onions Principle

I never miss important opportunities to reflect. I know this sounds unusual for businesspeople like me: Usually action-oriented people don't stop to reflect on what's happening. But that's how you lose focus. You then miss the chance to be honest with yourself (know where you are strong and where you need to improve) and fall short on awareness of how you are delivering on your promises.

• You need to be looking for ways to ask the right kind of questions in the right way. I know no better place to make sure everyone understands the value that they're giving than in a meeting with everyone together and participating—and grading each other.

Throughout my business career, in semiannual meetings of my companies and departments ranging from 3 to 700 people, I have held what I call "midterms" in which the entire team and I grade every person or group and have them grade themselves. I never tell them when it is coming—so no one can collude or rehearse—but I do make sure all the questions are fair and that we all have in front of us the results being graded. Then, we look over the last six months to see how far we've come, where we stand, and where we're going, and evaluate the processes we used. We review every item one by one, and then we stop and I ask them to grade themselves. After they grade themselves, I ask if everybody is satisfied with that grade and what grade the audience would give. Finally, I give my grade.

This is as close as you get in business to standing naked in front of a mirror. And whatever might be happening in

America's classrooms, there is rarely any grade inflation here. Not only that, the grading really varies. The people being graded are often much harder on themselves than I am in general topics like whether we were delivering on our promises, profits, net expectations, and market penetration. People might give themselves a C, the rest of the room will give them a B, and I give them a B+.

But the goal is not to be self-effacing or even to get a high grade. *The goal is awareness:* to look at where things were when we started and get valuable feedback that we can use to make it even better next time. It is about looking for the right tools. Because other people can help you know what you don't know.

Simply put, aspire to know what you don't know—and make sure you know what you do know—every single time. Think of yourself as a beginner and revel in the challenge of each initiative and sale as if it is something new. Every time you succeed, don't stop at reflecting on your success and then devolve into a routine that dismisses asking the biggest and most important questions the next time through. Win the RACE by asking and answering each question from this chapter again and again, adding new and different ones to suit your business or industry's needs as you do.

> **Am I Willing to Be a Beginner?**

And always ask yourself, "What don't I know?" That's how you keep Johnny Vegas Syndrome at bay. That's how you avoid becoming obsolete as you evolve through different stages of growth. That's how you make sure you don't think you know it all the next time through.

But Remember: Even the Best-Made Shoe Can Step In...

The Chicago meeting was big, and I was leading my team to the all-hands-on-deck in-person presentation. No "liver and onions" here: We had prepared every step of the way, asking the right questions and understanding what our potential client wanted and needed. We had anticipated other questions and prepared answers. The presentation was strong and we all knew our parts. I felt good—and looked good in my new black suit. (Okay, it was from JCPenney, but I still looked good for me back then.)

I was actually relaxed as Tami drove me to the airport with our baby daughter, Lindsey, in the backseat. I was smiling as I kissed Tami good-bye and took Lindsey out of her seat and gave her a big hug. I handed her back to Tami making one last goofy dad face for a smile and rushed off to the gate to meet my team. The flight was on time. I was psyched. I found my seat, took off my jacket, and lay back.

Yeah, maybe I had a little Johnny Vegas going on, but nothing wrong with a little bravado. Confidence is key, and I was not infected: We were ready as we walked in that room. And the presentation seemed to be working better than I expected. My confidence grew as the people at the table looked at me with rapt attention and even smiled. As I walked back and forth to the screen to integrate our graphics, I thought, "I've got them. I can tell. I can see them watching me and hanging on every single word." As we headed to the lobby, I was jazzed. I turned to the team and high-fived them. "Did you see that? Did you see the way they looked at me as we presented? Nice work! They wanted us. I just know it."

That's when the team said, "Jeff, take off your jacket." I did. "Now, take a look at the back."

The spit-up stain was four inches wide and ran from my shoulders down to the middle of the jacket. I knew now that every single time I turned around, it had been Lindsey's breakfast not my deft presentation skills that made them smile.

No matter how much you follow my advice, stuff is going to happen. You cannot prepare for or prevent everything, and you'll drive yourself crazy trying to—or worse, paralyze yourself into inaction. You need to let your people and even yourself fail. At the very least, learn to admit mistakes without qualification or excuses. How would it sound if I said after I saw my jacket, "Stupid baby vomit! Why did I have kids? Why did I have to hug my little girl good-bye? If I didn't have kids, I would have been perfect!" Better to learn from what happened (you can be sure I check every part of me front and back before I enter a room today), and make sure your team does too.

> **No One Is Going to Die When Stuff Happens, So Get Over It**

Of course, we won that business in Chicago. Because even when stuff happens, it still often turns out okay. And even when it doesn't, it's okay too. We don't have lives in our hands, just a small part of life. And as long as your mistakes don't come from sloppy thinking or preparation—as long as you don't lose before you begin and have the confidence to lead—you'll rarely end up with liver and onions on your plate...unless that's what you wanted there in the first place!

Chapter Five

Adding and Getting Value

What Works and What Does Not

Tami and I were having dinner with friends at the posh '21' Club. It was our first time in this New York City landmark restaurant. We had just sat down and started catching up when Tami saw a waiter delivering a captivating cocktail to another table.

"What's that?" she asked us. We all looked: Tall and purple and sparkling, it looked like something she'd love. But none of us was sure exactly what it was. We decided to ask the waiter when he came back.

Minutes later, the waiter appeared again, but before we could ask, he set the same cocktail down in front of Tami with a flourish. "Kir Royal: Champagne and crème de cassis," he said. "Compliments of the house."

Tami was thrilled (and enjoyed her cocktail immensely), and we all decided to order drinks. Then, Tami saw the same waiter with the supersonic hearing deliver a fantastic-looking dish to another table. She called him over and asked, "What's that?"

"Steak tartare," he said. Tami thanked him.

Minutes later, the waiter delivered a small portion to her. "Compliments of the house."

I couldn't help myself. I grabbed the waiter, "What's a Mercedes?"

"Don't push it," he said.

So, the waiter didn't get me that Mercedes. He did, however, get a huge tip for outstanding service punctuated by those small moments of added generosity. Through him, '21' had done with us what every business must strive to do: add value to a customer's experience without adding much (if any) real cost. Whatever the tiny impact giving my wife a free drink and a small sample of food had on '21''s bottom line, it was easily offset by the food and drink we ordered that night. We were satisfied customers willing to pull out our wallets and contribute to '21''s profits, and we became repeat customers when we returned to New York City.

You probably have restaurants and other businesses like '21' in your life: places that you love going to because they treat you well. It doesn't matter if their spoons are greasy or silver or if they serve food at all; from a simple hello and welcome back when you walk in the door to delivering something extra while you are there,

> **Thoughtfulness Tops Cleverness Every Time**

they always add a little value to every experience—and you love being treated that way. They make you feel great, and their thoughtfulness stays with you long after you walk out the door. These are the places you come back to again and again.

As we learned in the last chapter, your business's value

proposition is linked to the quality you deliver not the price you charge—to building your reputation and character not generating dollars and cents. Even Wal-Mart's customers connect value to the fact that they can find what they need under one roof, not just the store's low prices. Thus, even when your business is breathing well, your marketing is solid, your sales closed, and your service finished, your work is not done. From the moment your customers walk in the door through the completion of the sale and then in between that sale and the next, you need to think constantly about adding value.

The opportunity is available to anyone, so stop making excuses that you just don't have the time. From small moments of added generosity to high-tech equivalents, finding ways to add value without adding cost is one of the simplest ways to connect with your customers—it is the definition of macro marketing on a micro budget. Not only that, your brand depends on it. Remember: A brand is more than something you put on a cow; it's a promise—one you must deliver to gain customers and keep them coming back and buying more. A great business has a clear value proposition in everything it does.

And once you think about adding value for your customers, think about it in terms of *getting* value in all parts of your business: We already discussed how to get more value from your employees; why not enlist your vendors in spreading your business's value proposition? Look at your sales, marketing, and advertising plans and ask hard questions about whether the value and sales you get justifies the cost, whether they allow you to do more than simply broadcast your message, and if they use traditional *and* new media models to work for your audience.

To add and get value in your business you need to know what works—and what does not—for you. Let's start with the little things.

Adding Value Without Adding Cost—It's the Little Things

After cleaning up and straightening out my New Horizons computer franchise, I felt good about our chances for success. We had an improved service that people needed, and now we looked like we knew what we were doing. We had a solid business and marketing plan for attracting customers, and we had incentives in place to bring in more of the best customers without compromising profits (like buy five training sessions get the sixth free). For some businesses, this might be enough, but I still needed a way to add a little more value to the experience and make a lasting impression on our customers.

After all, what happens when they leave? Maybe today they post a review on Yelp or another review site. Maybe they keep their promise to refer us to another company or offer us a testimonial for our website. But that's not added value—that's important but it's not something that connects us in a lasting way. The problem with technology is that as much as it connects us faster and easier than ever before it is also so much air: Miss a post or click delete and it is gone. I needed something they would take with them to make them feel special and build our community.

I settled on presenting every person who "graduated" from our training programs with a fun diploma and picture of their group in front of our company sign as a keepsake.

I'm not sure how many people kept them, but they sure did smile when they received them, and I bet more than a few hung them in their offices, offering us a bit of free advertising and connecting us to them for as long as it stayed on the bulletin board. (As you know, those pictures tend to stay there for a long time.) Soon, I added a few other items like free chili dogs on Fridays, working with a local business downstairs for a special deal. Little cost (about fifty cents each), perhaps some indigestion, but a lot of added value.

Adding value can also tie directly into sales incentives. When I owned my printing company, I always knew when customers had not placed their usual orders for stationery or invoices—items that usually got used up in the course of a year. So, I contacted them and said, "Hey it has been a year since you ordered stationery, and based on your previous use, it's probably time to order more. Oh and if you order this week, you get a free box of embossed envelopes." They didn't know these envelopes cost me next to nothing compared to the overall order, but just like at '21' a little can seem like a lot when it is delivered by someone who clearly listens to you, remembers your business, and thoughtfully considers what else you might like to order.

The point of this story isn't the product (digital processes alone have replaced a lot of the need for paper invoices and stationery in many businesses). The point is the process of adding value. In fact, today, companies like Netflix and Fingerhut pay millions for algorithms that help them infer what a customer might like or need to buy based on purchases and other customer details. Small businesses need to make sure they pay close attention to their customers. Thinking this way and executing on the ideas is how they build a reputation for value with their customers: *by actually valuing them.*

Simply put, customers are not numbers to small businesses—they are people and that is your innate advantage over the big boys. And those customers expect you to know them and their business as well as they do. In Chapters 8 and 9, we will see how to sell to these customers on a one-to-one basis using a mixture of traditional and new media. But before that, ask yourself:

• What can you do to better know and track your customers and add more value without adding cost? It is not about being clever or sophisticated as much as it is smart, and it gets you thinking about the value proposition of any marketing and sales you do.

For example, my hometown hair salon does all the basic things well: tries to schedule appointments when customers pay and calls customers to remind them of the appointments they make. It sells all the grooming products the stylists use. But what would it cost them to add a little more value? What if I fail to make an appointment when I leave (in other words they forgot to ask for the sale)? How hard is it to put in a system that tracks when regular customers like me were last there and remind them to stay in touch and stay groomed? Maybe give me a call or send me a postcard or an e-mail saying it's been five weeks and I might be getting pretty shaggy? And how much would it cost them the next time I'm there to ask what my favorite beverage is and then have it ready for me next time I come? (I do love a Diet Mountain Dew.) How great would it make me feel if I got a hot towel spiced with tea tree oil to refresh myself when I'm done (and of course have those towels and oil for sale at checkout along with the grooming products)? I guarantee I will not only remember their thoughtfulness and generous spirit—and not flinch if they charge me a little more than other salons—but also come back again.

- Do you know how much I love the warm cookies they serve at the Doubletree? (I eat them with a big glass of whole milk—if you're going to do it, you have to go all the way.) I think about them when I am at other hotels—how's that for a lasting impression?
- Gans Ink uses Tootsie Rolls; they put some into cases of ink they send to print shops. I have seen people race each other like a roller derby to open the case of ink for the Tootsie Rolls. Think that helps spread goodwill?
- The woman who cleans my house folds the end of the toilet paper down as an added touch, and my son forbids anyone to use the bathroom until he gets to use that first sheet. Think we all don't notice what a special job she does?

In *Yes! 50 Scientifically Proven Ways to Be Persuasive*, Noah J. Goldstein, Steve J. Martin, and Robert B. Cialdini analyze the importance of what I call adding value without adding cost in great detail. Using a combination of social psychology, pop culture, and scientific research to understand the essence of persuasion, they help companies hone

> **Why Are There No M&M's on Your Counter?**

their marketing strategies by showing how "the subtle addition, subtraction, or substitution of a word, phrase, symbol, or gesture can significantly influence consumer behavior." They have even more great examples of how big-picture marketers add value with little things like Post-its and after-dinner mints to make customers feel special.

Like me, these authors know that smart business owners are always selling something, and the more personal connection the better and bigger the sale. They know it is more important than ever to make your customers happy. Remember: Customers will go anywhere because of price. But they can't go anywhere to be happy—that's how adding value without adding cost can help you bulletproof your business in good times and bad.

The problem comes when we undermine those connections and sales in the name of volume or value, allowing people to take advantage of us. An example of the former (volume) is competing on price and the file cabinet story from Chapter 3. My fullest understanding of the consequences of attempting to offer what I thought was value without seeing the costs came on a rainy Saturday when I was twenty-nine years old.

Adding Cost Without Adding Value—When Bad Things Happen to Good Festivals

To celebrate the South Dakota state centennial, I decided to put together a three-day folk festival that would feature performances, food, and a small trade show with local vendors. When I say "I," I mean it: I arranged for the financing—a large chunk of it from my own pocket—and for my staff of sixty to run it. I was only twenty-nine years old at the time with a small-but-growing business that was doing well, though cash was tight as we were expanding our services. But I wanted to do this for my business and my community. With strong marketing, advertising, and word of mouth, we expected 200,000 people over the three days. The profit possibilities were not huge, but the value my business would get in connections, exposure, and goodwill we could leverage through our expansion was high.

So, I expected to get value from the festival; that's good. What I didn't expect was rain—lots of it, nonstop, for the first day and a half. Anticipated attendance was off by tens of thousands. The vendors were miserable.

Now, a few vendors at trade shows always bitch and moan: My booth is too far from the door, I don't like who is next to me, my whites aren't white enough...Only this time, I did more than listen to them and try to calm their nerves. I also made a huge mistake. Instead of saying, "Listen, stuff happens. There is still time and the weather is getting better.

> **Giving or Offering Money Back Does Not Add or Deliver Value**

Let's look at everything when it is done and see how we met your expectations." I kept on talking and in a misguided effort to deliver value I added, "And if you don't like what's going on and what you're getting, we'll give you your money back."

A line formed immediately.

Now, some of these vendors really believed they weren't getting and would never get the traffic they needed and thus felt they would not get the value they expected. Even with great traffic during the second half of the festival, they knew they would have trouble breaking even and did not have faith enough to hold out. Others had gone beyond worry—they had invested all they had for the booth, staff, and setup and were freaking out. But some were just followers who saw the line forming and thought, "I might as well get in on this too." And some saw a naked opportunity to walk all over the idiot who opened his mouth and gave everything back.

• These are exactly the types of people who will take advantage of you in any business when you give money back in the name of value—especially if you do so before you have any idea if your value proposition has been fully communicated.

In the end, more than half the people came to get their money back. What was worse, I didn't *have* the money to cover these refunds. My own business was cash-constrained by the festival and our expansion. Even before the event started, I was worried about being so deep in the hole. I was scared. I had a skinny profit margin and big expenses. I actually had to track down my banker at a concert on the fairgrounds and ask for an extension on some payments so I knew the checks would clear.

Did I know I screwed up? Of course I did! I knew it as soon as I let the words slip from my mouth. If I could have kicked my own butt, I would have. I also knew while none of this was tied to my business's value proposition, I still could not compromise my personal value proposition. I needed to do the right thing and stand behind my choices, no matter how utterly stupid. Besides, I was a little scared of a few vendors based on what they sold (if they could do that to an animal, what were they going to do to *me*?).

Sure, I knew people were taking advantage of me, but I had no one to blame but myself for thinking people wouldn't take advantage of an opportunity to cash in on my misplaced notion of value. Still, I wanted them to know I knew and could live with myself. I delivered the checks personally, looking each person dead in the eye when I did. I wanted them to know that I had faced myself in the mirror, and if they could, then what else could I do except make sure the tax people knew they got a refund for the booth? I can only worry about how I do business—and make sure I add and get value in all I do.

Getting Value: Don't Give Away the Meat

Headquartered in my hometown of Sioux Falls, South Dakota, John Morrell & Co. is the largest meatpacking plant in the United States. Its brands are available and beloved nationwide. More than twenty years ago John Morrell taught me the best lesson I ever learned about getting value: "Don't give away the meat." This lesson and my advice to never compete on price are the two most important messages I have.

The story begins at the annual Easter Egg Hunt hosted by local Sioux Falls businesses. The hunt had grown with my help from a fun little event for hundreds into a fun huge event for thousands of parents and kids featuring entertainment and prizes that everyone looked forward to. But we needed someone to provide the food. That's when I dialed up John Morrell & Co.—their hot dogs were already well-known, and the business was one of the largest in the state.

I figured this was a no-brainer. Our event had a clear value proposition, which I presented to the company: This was their community and audience, and they would reach them directly. The company would get signage and promotion in all our materials. It was easily worth the couple of thousand dollars or so it would cost John Morrell & Co. to give us the 10,000 hot dogs we needed. I knew the company had to be interested. And sure enough, John Morrell agreed to speak with me. I didn't waste any time.

"Can you give me 10,000 hot dogs?" I asked.

"No," he said.

This moment was one of the few times in my life I was at a complete loss for words. I knew he could afford to give the hot dogs to me, but I could also tell he was dead serious. He let me squirm for a bit and then he continued.

"No, but I'll give you a check so you can buy them at retail."

Now, I was confused. "What are you, crazy? I'm giving you an opportunity to provide them at cost and you're gonna give me a check to buy them at retail?"

"Yeah, Jeff, we don't give the meat away."

Instantly his words sunk in: *He doesn't give the meat away.* He told me that he doesn't give the meat of what he sells away. And from that day forward, neither did I. Whatever my "meat" is—printing, PR services, computer trainings, photography, rental properties—I never give that away.

Never Give It Away

In fact, John Morrell did more than teach me a lesson and give me a check that day: He made his customers very happy too by spreading the money around. He got the value he needed, I got the donation we needed, and those retailers got the business they needed.

• Give it away and you are nothing to the customer: If you give the meat of what you sell away—not a taste or a sample but the actual product or service—you completely devalue that product or service and eliminate the chance of creating greater demand and getting real value.

Viewed this way, giving what you sell away actually costs you more than, well, what it costs. At the very least, it means less fog on the mirror. Give them a check, give them gift certificates to redeem, but trust me, the moment you give it away someone will come back every single day asking you for more.

Okay, So How Do I Evaluate If I Am Getting Value?

Maybe in this one instance, the recent changes in sponsorships by big companies can serve as examples for the little guys. Many people still use the term *Kodak Moment* to describe the instant something special happened in their lives—whether they captured it on film or not. This is what made big brands and the world's premier sporting event, the Olympics, a perfect match for more than a century starting with the first modern Olympics in 1896. Perhaps in the age of cameras and film, the investment paid dividends with lots of product to sell and real "Kodak Moments" to snap.

Note, I said made (past tense). That's right: today, many companies have dropped their sponsorship of the Olympics, and not because the price tag got too high but because the value proposition the Olympics offered was not there anymore. These same companies also dropped their long-standing NASCAR sponsorships and similar sporting events. In the age of digital, most businesses must realize:

- It is not fast enough: Fast-moving, digital companies need to get messages out constantly, and an event that happens every two years just does not work in that way.
- A traditional sponsorship model is broadcast in a narrowcast world and often broadcast to the wrong audience: To sponsor a major sporting event, you buy a category or ad time to have your logo and commercials and taglines displayed on networks, in stadiums, etc. But if your most important customers are businesses, they are a fraction of the millions who watch and attend these consumer events.
- It offers no control: In this sponsorship model, the event controls the proverbial horizontal and vertical. There is often no room for creativity or innovation—to control how it is sold and sell it using a blend of media. A company provides the content and logos; they show it.

Don't get me wrong: The Olympics' platform can still offer a value proposition for businesses like McDonald's and Coca-Cola—companies that sell products that the Olympics' customer still consumes. The problem is not sports either. Whether it's a neighborhood Little League team, a citywide charity event, the Olympics, or anything in between, sports still appeal to businesses, and direct sponsorship of a sports team or special event will likely remain a staple of many businesses' marketing and advertising. And some traditional models can still offer value for certain businesses. This is why Citibank could justify the value in putting its name on the New York Mets' new ballpark while accepting government bailout money.

Unfortunately, in the age of select/deselect, this traditional form of marketing offers a decreasing return on investment as customers develop ever-stronger mental filters that "blind" them to the message you have placed on the uniforms, programs, game car, etc., especially if that's the only place your message is broadcast. I am not saying buying space on an outfield wall or on the third turn at a speedway is always a bad idea. Please support your hometown team and local Little League. But big companies are now learning what smaller companies must know to survive: The value proposition of events (sporting or otherwise), not to mention any advertising or marketing campaign that relies on broadcast models, can be way off.

> **Do the Scale and Value of What You Are Doing Align?**

To determine if you are getting value for your business with an opportunity, ask yourself three questions:

1. Does the usual broadcast model work for your audience?
2. What does your participation allow you to do beyond broadcast your message?
3. How much do you have to sell to justify the cost?

Does the Usual Broadcast Model Work for Your Audience?

Chances are, no. Businesses must use every sales and marketing tool they have—networking, data collection and management, customer relations management, a blend of technologies (conventional and digital)—to create programs and messages designed for one person that will be welcomed and read by that person. But the keys to understanding whether you are getting value come down to scalability of the idea (being able to scale a program up or down in size depending on your need and its success) and personalization. Because when communication is personalized, response rates go up *and* are faster (and cost less per lead), orders increase, and revenue and profits rise. Broadcast alone rarely offers this.

- Create or shift your money to the opportunities that are scalable, and target individual customers on the most personal level.

What Does Your Participation Allow You to Do Beyond Broadcast Your Message?

For maximum value and effectiveness, businesses need to go beyond sponsorship and increase the return on investment by creating a new style of marketing programs (sports or otherwise) that offer a more complete experience. This is the same reason why smart businesses are turning away from TV ads and simple product placement (as viewers are growing increasingly blasé about seeing their favorite celebrities drinking Coke or driving Jeeps).

Today, for any business, maximum value comes from making your message an integral part of the program rather than a gimmick.

To replace big-ticket sponsorships, companies have gotten more creative in extending their brands and making sure their sponsorships stretch their money over time. For example, FedEx worked with the PGA Tour to create the FedEx Cup, the first men's professional golf playoff system. And since business owners and managers are members at the places these tournaments are played, FedEx also effectively narrowcast its message. Companies like FedEx know whatever extra manpower is needed to manage and run these kinds of sponsorships, they almost always end up generating more and costing less than events like the Olympics.

Why would any of this matter to a smaller business? Because we applied the same principles in a much more scaled down form to the Sioux Falls Easter Egg Hunt, and I took control of an opportunity to make it work for me. The goal in any sponsorship or event opportunity is to take control of the physical and virtual space for yourself. Look for ways to create

> **The Goal Is Control:**
> **Remember to Lead**

opportunities to generate awareness much greater than you would get by simply sponsoring it.

Don't have millions of dollars to work with the PGA? Sponsor the ninth hole of the most popular golf course in town for a month and track the best scores or longest drives for a prize. Help people take pictures and talk about it by tying it to all the media you can, especially your own website or web campaign. Give your audience a chance to interact and spread the word for you. This is where innovation and control really pay off.

- Narrowcast models are time-consuming to create and negotiate, use several media, and have many moving parts and details to account for but are still almost always cheaper—even accounting for the extra time and labor—than broadcast models.

How Much Do You Have to Sell to Justify the Cost?

Going back to what I said before about how giving away the meat always costs you more, the main reason is no opportunity is just about selling the product and service. Time, promotional materials, travel and setup, signage, and the numerous other line items needed to activate the plan must be factored into any budget and usually amount to double your buy-in cost. So, if you spend $20,000 for the opportunity, you had better budget $40,000 to activate that opportunity.

For opportunities and sponsorships on larger scales, activation might not be quite that much (perhaps $20 million to activate a $50 million plan), but on any scale it's still a lot of money. That's why those vendors at the folk festival were nervous—they had spent more than just a booth fee to have the chance to pitch their products and services. To justify this cost, answer the fundamental question about value: Can I generate this amount (about three times the buy-in cost) in sales or other value offered (like the folk festival was supposed to do)?

- But whatever your sales expectations are, stuff happens. So, your decision to buy in should be made on the overall value you will get.

Measurement of the value you get beyond sales used to be in ears and eyeballs, now it's hearts and minds, but however you measure (and you *must* measure), keep in mind the best buy is not always the cheapest. Just as competing on price will destroy your business, always choosing the lowest price for an advertising or marketing plan or in choosing any vendor might too.

I'm not saying the most expensive people are always the best value in sales and marketing; I'm saying the best value for your business may not be determined by price. Sometimes low cost simply means cheap and low impact. To keep the mirror fogging, your business needs strong revenues and profits. The most expensive people might offer you the best value if they generate the right exposure to build the biggest revenues and profits, whereas the cheaper vendor could just drive your costs down and cost you by offering considerably lower revenues and profits.

Don't fall for the fancy social media pitches that claim to reach millions at the click of a button if they are not targeting and reaching the right people. The print guy might be offering you a better value. You'd be surprised how many people dismiss this even when the numbers are right in front of them. Because print is not sexy—print can be expen-

> **Don't Always Listen to the Cheap Guy**

sive and time-consuming to produce. But if a print campaign offers you $13 in sales for every dollar that you spend and the social media campaign offers you only a three-to-one ratio, should that be of interest to you? Yes, you might be able to save money with other platforms, but spending more to get greater return can be worth it if it means directly reaching your customers and getting them to *buy*.

• Any marketing or sales program that targets customers on a one-to-one basis, regardless of the media involved, is going to be expensive. But if you're getting bigger sales and reaching exactly the customers you want to reach, then it will be worth it. The key here is relevance—more relevance, more value.

You Can't Always Get What You Want, But You Can Make Sure You Get What You Need

"Hey Mike, it's Jeff...Whatcha doing this weekend?"

"Nothing!" he said with anticipation. "Got a job for me?"

Mike was the copier technician for my print shop. He did all my repairs and he did them really well. I wasn't calling to see if Mike wanted to go bowling or hunting or grab a beer; he knew it and was delighted. I was calling to see whether he and his family wanted to stay at the Holiday Inn across the street from my shop.

When my quick print shop knew we had a high-speed, high-volume job, we tried to arrange to do it on a weekend. Jobs like that were often too big for my small shop to do on a daily basis, but the jobs were important to our customers and highly lucrative for us ($5,000 and up with big profit margins). So, whenever I could, I would schedule jobs like those over the weekend in shifts. And then, I would plan for something to go wrong, because something is always going to happen, and I was going to need a repair guy. But where was I going to find a repair guy on short notice on the weekend?

Across the street at the Holiday Inn.

For the cost of a couple of rooms (downtown week-end discount rate) for Mike, his wife, and the two kids, and a few meals, I got what I needed in minutes. Mike would cross the street at 2:00 a.m. in his pajamas and fix my machine if he had to. And why not? He was having a great time. He was happy. Half the time, these jobs came during the winter. Have you *been* to South Dakota in February? He had to travel a few frigid steps for a repair he would have had to make from a much farther distance while fighting frostbite. And my business made him a hero to his family as they ordered room service and used the heated swimming pool, while all their friends tried not to freeze on the ice.

This wasn't adding value without adding cost, but it was a lesson in getting value from all parts of your business: We took care of Mike, and he took care of us. I don't believe in zero-sum games, and this was the definition of a win-win for my business. So why don't more businesses think about their vendors and suppliers this way?

As you know, I see trusting and valuing the people who work for you as an essential part of strong mirror-fogging leadership. But your job as a leader is to keep *all* the people working with you (not just for you) focused on your value proposition and building your

> **Treat Your Vendors and Suppliers Like Customers**

bottom line—that should include your vendors and sup-pliers. In fact, by thinking of Mike and treating him the way I did, he was almost working for us. When he did a repair job on a copier for a business, whom do you think he suggested for their bulk jobs? If he saw the competition's boxes on a desk, do you think he'd hesitate to ask if they knew about us?

These days we try to squeeze any advantage we can out of even our closest associates. Stop. Just like your employees and customers, make your suppliers and vendors part of your team. Share your dreams with them and listen to theirs. Think about adding value with them too like inviting them to happy hours or company outings or sending a few Tootsie Rolls with their check. You may never need the relationship the way I did when I owned my print shop, but if the time comes, you can't use what you don't have.

Truth is, my vendor story and all the stories in this chapter are about looking for value through and beyond our customers. Smart companies have learned that they need to add and get value in everything they sell and do and everyone they work with or for to thrive. With businesses needing to confront changes and new demands faster than ever, those games are far too common. Businesses must be prepared to relearn and reevaluate what they know on a continual basis. This is how we adapt...or die.

Chapter Six

Adapt or Die

Losing After You Begin

We were on safari in Africa when we spotted a lone antelope darting across the plain. Graceful and forceful, it ran with breathtaking speed. Moving in a straight line, it literally left everything in a cloud of dust. We felt nothing could ever catch it...until it ran full speed into the only tree on the plain and landed right in front of two hungry lions lounging in the shade. Lunch: food delivered to the paws of the lions as they lay there just waiting.

Okay, this never happened to me. It's a viral video of unknown origin that I first used at a sales conference when I worked at Cenveo (one of the largest visual communication companies in North America). Just search the web for "two lions antelope video" and you will find it. I know it's not real, but it is funny; for years, I used it at the start of presentations, and it never failed to get a laugh. But the meaning I find in the video is no joke: *Adapt or die— learn to change course and realize the "food" will no longer come to us.*

You see I find fault with the antelope *and* the lions—they

127

are both failures in adaptability. It may seem that the lions "win" in this video—the food does come to them. After all, most people focus on the failure of the antelope: Even with only one tree to avoid, the antelope failed to shift course and made itself into convenience food. But if the kings of the jungle, like the kings of any business big or small, fast or slow, keep on waiting they will perish too.

Perhaps the food used to come to us in business—or that's what people like to believe. Ah, the allure of setting up your own shop. If you build it they will come, right? No! There are no fields of dreams in business. Trust me, I live in South Dakota, right next to Iowa, and no one I know goes there for anything except corn and pigs.

Okay, I'm exaggerating. I love Iowa. But no business there or anywhere is going to survive on dreams alone. Simply put, many businesses will lose and fail. As cited in the *New York Times*, a 2009 study by the *Monthly Labor Review* reported that just over 31 percent of businesses started in the second quarter of 1998 were still in business in the same quarter ten years later. Of course, many of those businesses should never have opened in the first place. Many lacked the capital or were too poorly financed to survive even if the food *did* fall on their plate. Others hung out their shingle and waited like those lions for the food to come to them. They failed the mirror tests and likely lost before they began by:

- Not knowing their pitch.
- Using outdated contacts and antiquated sales materials.
- Relying on a broadcast approach instead of a narrowcast one.

- Having unreasonable expectations.
- Treating all prospects or customers or employees the same.
- Displaying a lack of urgency in sales process.
- Failing to make an offer.

Sure, some of these problems only become apparent after you begin, but the proverbial seeds of failure were sown long before. For example, say you are a preferred customer of an airline or grocery store or any business that should know something about you, and they value your business for its sheer volume. How does that business make you feel special? Too often they don't; they treat you the same as everyone else. They just wait for the food to come back to them. Big businesses cannot afford to do this for long; small businesses cannot afford to do this at all.

But what about the businesses that succeeded for years, perhaps decades, and then failed? The same *Monthly Labor Review* study showed what most business owners already know: Survive four or five years and your chances of success increase considerably. But success is not a lifetime guarantee. Just because you did not fall victim to the "lose before you begin" mistakes, adjusted your antelope's course, and did wait for the food to come to you, you can still lose.

The late Sam Kinison had a joke about people starving in Africa. He wondered why all of them were in the desert. Nothing grows in the desert, he said: Move to where the food is! That's clearly politically incorrect advice for Africans

> **We Must Adapt and Change ... Constantly**

but perfectly correct advice for businesses: A business-as-usual approach will eventually kill you. No matter who you are in business right now—the speedy antelope that never changes course or the mighty but passive lion—you must adapt...or die.

I don't care if you sell submarine sandwiches or actual submarines; the business environment is changing, and you must adapt to survive. Like the second mirror test, this all goes back to Darwin and his survival of the fittest theory—there were certain animals that failed to adapt to survive. These days, small businesses must compete with everyone, everywhere. So, how do you grow sales in a business environment that strips even the most venerable companies of their business models and their very reasons for being? How do you grow with economies so global that local stores are harmed by events that take place half a world away? How do you speak to a country where groups we used to call minorities now often make up majorities yet still have distinct interests, languages, and cultures? You use the mirror tests as a foundation, and then:

- Understand how you fit into the realities of your industry and your customers now *and* in the future.
- Always have the contrarian voice in your business asking what you don't know.

Do this and you'll have what I call an "adapt-or-die mentality." With it, you will be able to change without destroying who you are. Without it, you can't hope to provide your customers with the value they need, let alone keep selling to them, and your business will eventually fail.

Of Razors and Reality: It's Not Your Father's Marketplace

Your company is in deep trouble. Everyone knows your brand name but time has rendered your product lines obsolete. You have missed chances to capitalize on new technologies. Your brand image makes people (particularly young people) shrug with indifference. Profits fall so dramatically that selling or dissolving the company sounds like a good idea...That was the story at many fallen corporate icons. Pan Am, RCA, Polaroid—a graveyard of American companies in a global cemetery.

These companies crumbled because they clung to business-as-usual approaches: too busy and distracted by success to think and act differently. After all, for more than a century, those companies had huge profit margins, tremendous worldwide brand recognition, and a long list of future orders. Why change? The biggest were the very definition of the "razor blade" model for business: It sold customers the "razors" they loved, and they kept coming back to buy the "razor blades" they needed to make the products work. But things change.

> **If Everyone Uses an Electric Razor, It Won't Matter That You Sell the Best Razor Blades**

Success in business moves in waves. From growing volume to reevaluation of priorities to optimization, all businesses will need to ride these proverbial waves, and obsolescence (a wipeout) can happen at any point. The goal is to look forward as you evolve—to use your adapt-or-die mentality and anticipate your customers' needs now *and* in the future. If you don't, your company will likely enter what Jim Collins in *How the Mighty Fall: And Why Some Companies Never Give In* calls the final stage of decline: "Capitulation to Irrelevance or Death."

Simply put, businesses that believe they are the best in the business—the crème de la crème—and then trade on that success alone are fooling themselves. Instead of balancing the big picture needs of tomorrow *and* today, they say things like, "We have always done it this way." In good times, they will get lazy and sloppy, relying for too long on consumer spending and fat profits and then flash and gimmicks to maintain the illusion of success before an inevitable collapse. I'm sure the guy who made the best buggy whips at the turn of the twentieth century still sold some to a rapidly shrinking market, but it didn't matter how much quality he had, his value (and company) was whipped by the advent of the automobile.

That's how companies didn't adapt. They entered the twenty-first century with a twentieth-century mentality, failing to realize they needed to do what any company with an adapt-or-die mentality must:

- Transform the business model and build a culture of innovation and winning.
- Introduce new products or ways of doing things even as you market the existing ones.
- Tap into new technologies.
- Shift your brand and its images, at the same time changing the organization and its operations in order to be a more modern and innovative company.
- Kill products and services that are not effective and anticipate future declines before it's too late.

Ultimately, mama did not take your Kodachrome or Pola-roids away—*people* did. They stopped buying film. In 1975, if you asked an audience who had bought a roll of film in the past month, every hand would go up. Now, how many people would raise their hands today? But back then, why change? Why adapt when there was no perceived need and the digital revolution was just hitting calculators. Sure, some hardcore users want those original products to stay, but most people (especially young people) move on. And continue to move on—fast. Technologies last for a few years at best these days, not decades. Anyone who remembers what the ink on a mimeograph smells like is surely over thirty in 2010.

I've worked with companies from tiny businesses in small markets to global brands and too often they fail to grasp these fundamental points of adapt-or-die. You can't wait years to capitalize on changes in the market. You can't stay analog while the world goes digital; you must adapt your business plans for the next big thing—sometimes literally. Custom Comfort Medtek has made top-quality medical furniture for clinics and labs since 1987. Over the years, they realized that even if more people were not entering a clinic, there was still "more" of them: obesity was becoming an epidemic. So, they started manufactur-ing wider chairs to handle these patients. They innovated with their existing products to introduce something new.

On the digital side, consider Apple and the iPod. While not the first to market, the iPod revolutionized digital music in 2001 with its small size and simple interface—two things every other player lacked. Despite a price tag that was and remains among the highest in the market and other small complaints, the iPod quickly won consumers and critics over and maintains a market share of around 70 percent.

But what Apple did next is the important lesson for any business: Even as the iPod became the industry standard and the company's dominant source of revenue (and unlike the antelope in the video), Apple continued to adapt. While it still innovated with its iPod line, Apple's entry into the smartphone category, the iPhone, as well as its latest notebook and desktop computers started to provide significant revenue streams.

My point isn't that you should go buy Apple. I could have easily picked IBM, Dell, or dozens of other examples from companies that fought back from the brink of irrelevancy. The point is the foundation of adaptation is built on attitude—a desire to change. It's not about a wholesale and systematic destruction of your principles, your products, or your people. It's about preparing for a different business environment while sustaining your existing environments.

And sometimes it starts with a fresh coat of paint. I'm serious. Sometimes the signs of decay in a company are so obvious the mood it creates prevents anyone from believing that change is possible. You know the feeling as a customer or an employee: You walk in the lobby or the front door and you sense that something isn't quite alive. In fact, you think it might be dying.

This is why I told you before that the first thing I do when I get to a company is clean. Maybe it's the military child in me, but I like to refresh everything when I arrive. In short, I want us to walk the talk—to look the part and for everyone to feel it. When I owned my print shop, I remodeled it to look like Xerox because those were the cutting-edge copiers we were using at that point and I wanted people to sense the connection when they walked inside. I do the same thing at the big companies I work for. I'll paint all the hallways, clean or rip up the carpets to uncover the beautiful floors, and replace all the old photos that line the walls for a cleaner, more modern look. I want us to *feel* like we can adapt while we take on the larger challenge of actually adapting.

Then, when you're done, get yourself some new clothes and a good haircut and look in the mirror and ask your bad self: "How can I know more of what I don't know?"

The Seven Adapt-or-Die Questions to Learn What You Don't Know

Awareness is key. Look around and what do you see? You must be obsessed as a business owner with the things that might put you out of business. You must drive out new processes and continuously make improvements to existing ones. You must avoid getting in that success "rut" and falling victim to hubris.

Start by getting a broader perspective. Learn what's happening in the industry through research and conferences and shopping the competition. Refresh your contact with your customers—not to sell them more but to anticipate what they might need in a few months or years. You never want to say, "Why didn't we think of that?" This means you had no idea something was even possible—that's failing to know what you don't know and losing *after* you begin. As opposed to saying, "I had no idea that was coming," which is losing before you begin, you failed to ask specific

The Adapt-or-Die Questions You Must Ask

questions about an existing product or service coming to market because you moved too quickly or thought sloppily.

To uncover what you don't know, ask yourself these questions about your business:

1. Are you still relevant today?
2. What might change?
3. Are you acting deliberately and decisively to confront the realities of reaching today's customer?
4. Why do you do things the way you do them—do you use your own processes?
5. How do other people do what you do?
6. Are there other ways to approach the problems you solve and the value you deliver?
7. Are you moving quickly to bring new products and services to market faster and are your response times as fast?

These questions are the best way I know to make sure that you are able to adapt. And honestly, you may not like the answers. Unless you anticipated and planned to be in transition (which is a form of adapting), if you are feeling less relevant and sense you cannot adapt to compete, you probably can't survive. *So, go ahead and die and go out on top.* Indeed, I have sold off several businesses from printing to cell phones because those companies could not compete as the market got bigger and was taken over by big business, or newer technologies made what I offered obsolete.

For better or worse, you must stand up and be willing to admit that there are things you do not know, that others may know, and that you need to know...no matter how much you already know now. In other words, don't be Johnny Vegas and believe your own press releases.

And then find a way to do as I do: Look for the great surprises in life. Be the contrarian—cause tension.

Contrary to Your Belief: How to Get at What You Don't Know

A few years ago, I was in London on business, and as I sat in my hotel, I started flipping through the channels on the TV. I love reality television (you think my being on *Celebrity Apprentice* was an accident?), and I settled on a UK design makeover show about a British hotel. Once a stylish jewel, the hotel was now fading like the owners themselves—comfortable still and charming perhaps but also run down. But the owners didn't see the faded drapes, worn carpets, and cracked ceilings. They thought it was great; it was their children who called the show for the makeover opportunity. The owners needed fresh eyes to see the necessary changes and then make them without losing the charm and comfort that made the hotel unique.

That's what a great contrarian does—and to adapt successfully you need to find one or learn to take the contrarian approach yourself.

When I join a big business, project, or political campaign, I always feel my job is to create tension. The best contrarians know how to take the lead and push people. Contrarians are not naysayers. They are people who can see the contrary position and imagine its value—for example, an investor who buys stock when most others are selling or vice versa. Contrarians look for opposing positions and challenge accepted wisdom. We stand up and say the emperor has no clothes and force those around us to react. *We don't just talk about the elephants in the room—we ride them and teach them a few tricks.*

But smart contrarians do not do all this for sport. We don't just "get into it." We won't compromise a company's values and diminish the promises it has made to its existing customers for the sake of change. Show me an example of a company that did that and survived. Our goal is to make a good thing better by knowing when to take risks and being able to stomach them.

That's what happens when I arrive. If a company needs to change its footprint, my cowboy boots make quite an impression. Even the team members who want change have never seen the likes of me literally ripping up the carpet. By the time I commission something like a video that mocks the old company approach, people within the company are already working with me to shake things up to show the company and its customers that our future is not in the past. I become their cheerleader—the person willing to take their initiative and push even harder.

As a contrarian, I like to be predictably unpredictable and always ask, "Can we change?" The biggest enemy of any business owner is complacency—getting so comfortable you either don't act when things are good or over-react when things are in a state of decline. If you can, hire someone or bring on a consultant you trust *while you're successful* to take a position against

> **Who Is Your Contrarian Voice?**

yours to help you avoid this. If there's no one but you, learn to do it yourself and take responsibility for being the innovator, especially when things are going great.

A simple way to do this is to shop your own business. Walk around and look at your business from the front of the counter as customers walk in. When I owned my print shop, I would make up an order and see how they handled it. Call during a busy time and see how long you're put on hold. Call your customer service people (or have someone do it and listen in) with a pretend problem and hear how they handle it. Click around your website and order your product or service and see how it is processed. And then do the same thing with your competitors.

Make sure you also use your advantages to help you anticipate what the possibilities are. When I was in the PR business for the graphics industry, my advantage was (and still is) my connections, so when I was at big events like trade shows I would look for ways to connect with everyone and hear what they had to say. For example, at a trade show in Chicago instead of getting a hotel room in town, I got one at the McCormick Place convention center, which is near nothing but the show and thus always has interminable taxi lines. I put together a cocktail reception in my room after the first day of the show and invited my most important contacts to join me and meet everybody instead of waiting with the riff raff for taxis. The information in that room was worth twenty times what I got on the convention floor.

Remember: The biggest fall is from the highest point. While one part of your business satisfies your customers' current needs and expectations, the contrarian rethinks it all from creating new value propositions to exploring new markets and specializations to repositioning your business. Think of it this way: Years ago mangoes, goat cheese, and sushi were distinctive, exotic specialties that commanded a premium. Today, every supermarket in the country offers them, so what's next for your customers?

And don't forget about your employees. If one of the biggest obstacles to achieving and the adapt-or-die mentality is getting the company—and its people—in the right mood, it is vitally important to develop company-wide alignment and agreement regarding your goals, methods, and metrics that work with your company's culture. Change is a heady thing, and putting the right processes in place helps you focus as those changes are made.

Wait, am I saying that Mr. Contrarian—who loves to be surprised—is committed to systematic processes? Yes, that's exactly what I am saying. I like order as much as I like change. When I come home, I don't want to go looking for my toothbrush. When I get to my office, I want to know my stapler is in the drawer where I left it with my favorite pair of scissors I've had for fifteen years. And when it comes time to change offices, I want to know that stapler is still there where I need it.

This is the same reason companies that have processes in place are best able to focus on the present *and* the future and deliver value even as they look for what they don't know. They will always succeed in the long run over companies that simply fly by the seat of their pants. They build a stable foundation for continual improvement on strong existing systems.

Whether you're building a team of motivated marketers,

smooth salespeople, or anything else, your first job is not getting them to sell the product; it's developing the process for them to work together. Whether the team consists of two or two thousand, if they're not working together, the game is over. It doesn't matter what your product is. It doesn't matter how many fancy charts and reports you have. It doesn't matter if you have slick brochures and a colorful website. If you don't have an enthusiastic, dedicated team all working from the same playbook, you're already lost.

Processes help the team get the existing work done efficiently and smartly so everyone can help take responsibility together for growth and change. They provide a frame for any mirror test and even change the mirror itself for the better. They allow your inner contrarian to adapt without destroying who you are.

Don't Change Who You Are...Just How You See Things

One of my favorite professional speakers, Scott McKain, has a great story that summarizes everything about adapt or die with one word: *cufflinks*. And whenever I think I might be getting too stuck in a particular way of thinking, I say to myself, "Cufflinks."

Scott was speaking in an out-of-the-way location, and as he was getting dressed he realized he forgot his cufflinks. He asked the front desk and they had none, neither did the small gift shop in the lobby.

> **You Can Know What You Don't Know**

There wasn't much around the hotel and it was getting late, so they suggested Scott try the big-box store down the street, but it had no cufflinks either. Did they know where he could get some? They were not sure but suggested another store down the block. No luck. By the third store, he was contemplating duct taping his cuffs or even using a stapler.

He returned to the hotel and reported his failure to the woman at the front desk who said, "Sir, why don't you just buy another shirt?"

Sometimes, the solutions we seek blind us to answers that are right in front of us—or the right questions to ask to get the answers we need. An adapt-or-die mentality not only makes us more competitive but also makes us see the bigger picture and appreciate different approaches. Fundamental shifts are not beyond your control. You can understand and prepare to handle what's about to happen in your business and industry. Take initiative to do the things you need to do to embrace, shape, and grow with those changes. I was asked to speak to MTV about social media and marketing—when I was almost fifty years old. I'm hardly MTV's demographic. I don't even look the part. But I act it. I had adapted quickly to use new marketing tools and technologies (like Twitter) to my and my company's advantage. I had moved to where the food was.

But adapting is not just about new technologies or becoming a "change agent." Adapt-or-die is about getting a *better* result, not just a different one. Changing for the sake of change can be more perilous for businesses than not adapting at all. It can make you forget who you are and what you stand for and destroy your value proposition. And it can make you take steps that ignore all the tools you have to sell your product or service, fail to reach the customer on the most personal level, and create plans that are bigger than necessary.

Part Three

Sell It

Chapter Seven

Scale Is the New Black

*Leverage Everything to Make Many
Out of One*

Tami and I fell in love despite our inability to see eye to eye...literally: I am six feet three inches tall, and she's five feet two inches tall. But fall in love we did and that meant I had to meet her great-grandmother, Grandma Agnes, who stood four feet ten inches tall on a good day. When the moment arrived, Tami led me over to her.

"Grandma, this is Jeff," said Tami, leaning over and yelling slightly. I was ready. I knew how much Grandma Agnes meant to Tami. I smiled big.

Grandma Agnes nodded as she looked up at Tami then turned and looked up at me and then back down to Tami and said, "Isn't he bigger than necessary?"

Fortunately, Tami thought I was just right. Unfortunately, too many marketing and sales plans are not; they *are* bigger than necessary. Even businesses that have passed the mirror tests and understand their value propositions make this mistake. In their efforts to deal with the realities of today's marketplace, deliver results quickly, and keep up with the latest cutting-edge technologies, too many businesses create expensive, bloated, unwieldy marketing plans that miss the big picture and forget what's really important: reaching their target audiences and constantly selling to them for the least amount of money and the greatest return.

This failure is unnecessary. And these last few chapters are here to help.

Sure, many of the old assumptions about how to market have been rendered useless by rapid changes in the economy, technology, and society, but all businesses must keep marketing to survive. They just need to:

- Do more with less.
- Relearn a big-picture approach to marketing that balances both common sense and innovation.
- Get away from the bigger-is-better broadcast approaches and throw-it-against-the-wall methods, and get back to best practices.
- Strive to create narrowcast plans that attempt to make one-on-one connections with their customers.
- Network and connect constantly.
- Be good stewards of precious marketing resources and use technology tools wisely.
- Build forward-looking campaigns that keep building step-by-step and expand as they succeed.

Of course, some business owners and marketers read the words *forward-looking campaign*, forget everything else, and then turn to electronic and social media and the latest technological advance for a quick fix. But like I said, there are no quick fixes in this book, no flashy promises or simple solutions. I certainly use social media such as Facebook or Twitter (see Chapter 9), and by the time this book comes out, I'll probably have explored more social media options and even started to use them—*but only if they deliver value and help me sell and market my business.*

You see, social media is only one tool in my marketing toolbox. Business owners should not get caught up in any medium if it does not work for their businesses. But social media is very compelling, sexy even. Its allure can make businesses ditch all other options for some misguided and strange alternatives, like rushing to establish a presence on Second Life before realizing everyone there doesn't have a First Life to begin with.

My definition of a forward-looking business is not based on how outside the pro-verbial box it thinks or how technologically savvy it is but how effectively it creates and scales its sales, marketing, and advertising campaigns. There's an old expression on the prairie: If you want to run with the big dogs, you got to learn to pee in the tall grass. In business, you must think and act big no matter your size. Any company can market wisely and market big no matter its budget. And while a company needs to be fast and relevant, it never needs to be bigger than necessary.

> **You're Only as Small Business as You Think You Are**

As I said before, scalability is the very definition of macromarketing on a microbudget. That's why I say scale is the new business black. A scalable approach is a commonsense way for even the smallest business to learn to:

- Leverage anything and everything it has.
- Ensure its marketing efforts can be multiplied through a step-and-repeat process.

- Try to make its business part of the story—getting away from traditional broadcast advertising or product placement.

Sure, you might think these are things you can do with a large business that you just cannot do with a small one of 2, 20, 200, or even 2,000 employees. Those big companies have more zeroes in their budgets, right? Absolutely. But I have spent decades acting like I'm bigger than I am, generating and scaling great marketing ideas to fit my companies' budgets, and this is what I have learned: That's all big companies do. There are no secret formulas. They are doing the exact same things and make the exact same decisions as small businesses do every day just on a larger scale. They just add (and subtract) more zeroes. And so can you.

Just Add Zeroes: The Foundation of Scalability

My professional career moved through small and medium-sized businesses of all kinds: PR, printing, politics, consulting, cell phones, and computers and eventually included some big *Fortune*-500-size companies. Along the way, people have had trouble understanding how all of my success was possible.

"How do you do it?" they ask. "How do you keep changing what you do from company to company?"

The answer is simple. "I don't change what I do. Not much, anyway. The same things I did in each of my small companies, I now do worldwide. I just added more zeroes."

In other words, I owe my success at big companies to

the same principle of scalability that I used when I ran my little print shop in Sioux Falls; I just scaled my ideas to suit the staff or budget I had. What I did with one employee, I then did with 10, 100, 100,000. Replace the word *employee* with *customer, dollar,* or *euro* and you get the point of scalability. That's what the big picture of business and marketing is all about for me: Just add or subtract zeroes.

It does not matter if the company is internationally known with megamarketing strategies and budgets the size of the GDP of a few developing nations. It's not like those companies have endless cash reserves or credit lines or did not need to improve what they were doing as their business changed and evolved. Remember, the primary business products being developed and sold by most digital companies didn't *exist* a few years before. If a business can change that fast, there's no way typical broadcast advertising and marketing plans can keep up. A business needs scalable marketing and sales plans that can grow, evolve, and adapt with the company.

In fact, I view the entire process of building a successful business as adding or subtracting zeroes through the following cycles or phases:

> **Everything Comes Back to Scale**

1. Introduction (establishing your presence)
2. Growth (building revenue or customers and trying to improve your margins)
3. Maturity (seeking and maintaining profitability)

Each phase begins with a period of acceleration or adding zeroes (as things move faster and begin to crystallize) followed by a period of deceleration or subtracting zeroes (in which you pull back as your business moves into the next phase). In the introduction phase, you add and invest more zeroes than you get back. You have more expenses and little revenue until your business "kicks in." So, you do everything you can to get that revenue. As you start the growth phase, you try to improve your margins by generating more zeroes (cash/revenues) through expansion, acquisition, or innovation. (You can tell when businesses start accelerating in the growth phase—that's when the owners buy a nicer car or take the more expensive vacation.) And finally, when that success has been achieved, you reach maturity and start to rationalize your growth; you think about what all the zeroes mean as you reevaluate your value proposition and adapt or die.

I like to look at marketing in my business against these same phases. In phase one, I'm no longer a one-man band planning the launch of my business. I'm out there. I'm trying to establish my abilities with my audience and build devout followers. I'm looking for customers. This is where you can get a militarylike scorched-earth mentality (extreme and deliberate destruction of anything that stands in your way—dominant market share at all costs). But watch out. A little scorched-earth mentality is needed to build confidence and fuel healthy ego. A full-on scorched-earth mentality in business can burn you—with your customers with whom you will fail to build a relationship and with your competition who will do anything to destroy you before you destroy everything in the name of generating revenue. (A price war is a kind of scorched-earth mentality.)

Think of it like being trapped in a brush fire. You can do two things to survive. You can run like hell in any direction. Maybe you'll outrun the fire. Maybe. That's the full-on scorched-earth mentality in business. A better solution is to run only as far as you need to get ahead of the fire, burn and stomp out a large circle of ground big enough for you to lie down in (with room to spare on all sides), and lie down. When and if the fire comes, your piece of scorched earth will protect you. With nothing to burn inside your circle, the fire goes around you and moves on.

When you are launching your business, you must have a laser-like focus on that little piece of earth in the fire. And you must try to connect directly and fully with your target customers in that area and then build on them. You do not want to "run like hell" — unrestrained or uncontrolled invest- **Do Not Overreach** ing in huge ineffective broadcast programs and marketing plans that you cannot hope to sustain. A business is far better off trying to get as many customers as it can within a contained and controlled area. As you succeed, be ready to add zeroes. Expand from one mile to ten, two miles to twenty. Go from targeting 100 customers to 1,000, then 1,000 to 10,000 as your business is established. That's what scale is.

• Control and own the ground around you first and capitalize on your success with more zeroes.

I know, this all sounds so simple, but time and again you will read about some small business that failed because they "overexpanded," "tried to do too much too fast," or "failed to start small." That is, they failed to take a scalable approach to their sales and marketing. Yet people still underestimate and dismiss me precisely *because* a scalable approach is so simple. They don't realize there's a "process" behind my "madness." Truth is, it's the best process I have.

I see everything I do as scalable in some way. For example, my list of what great sales leaders do is a natural scale or progression:

- Set a vision for sales success.
- Ensure alignment between company's objectives and customer needs.
- Deliver no matter what.
- Build and manage your own excellence model; follow best practices.
- Hold people and yourself accountable for results.
- Celebrate success with reward and recognition programs.
- Anticipate the future.
- Look for innovation in your own and within different market and vertical segments.

On the marketing side, so much of what I learned came from my experience with my little print shop in Sioux Falls. When my print shop started doing "spec books" for an architecture firm's jobs (200-plus-page inspection manuals and blueprints for the firm and its construction teams), I knew I was on to something good. These jobs cost $2,000 a pop, more than ten times my average big job. After I successfully completed a couple, I wondered if other architects needed this service and started to reach out *personally* to firms around Sioux Falls. I found a vertical market and scaled within it.

When we owned the market for our services in the

metro area of Sioux Falls, I looked at my capacity and travel time and wondered if I could expand my offerings to a 15- to 20-mile radius of Minnehaha County. So, I sent my sales and marketing materials to a list of 1,000 similar businesses in addition to the 100 businesses I already did regular business with downtown. I added a zero to the smaller group to sell more based on the success we had already experienced with similar businesses.

When I met regularly with a group of small business owners—a sort of mini board of directors for my shop (which had grown dramatically since I took it over)—I stopped talking about being a part of the $1 million sales club and started talking about the $1 million net club. I wanted to add zeroes on my top line and my bottom line—to think about profitability not just revenue growth.

I'm not saying these are the only examples or that they will work for you or that scaling everything will work for every business. Heck, if black does not work for you, don't wear it. But you need to know that what I did is the exact same thing any successful national and worldwide company does with its marketing; they just do it with more zeroes.

Building scale is often hard work—a lot harder than a quick fix like buying a list and blasting out a few million e-mails and then hoping for some response. But honestly, we make marketing tougher than it is. If you are one of those marketers or business owners overthinking your plans (again, no one is going to die so go for it) or clinging to bigger than necessary approaches, try a scalable approach. Trust me, I wouldn't work this hard if the return on my investment wasn't almost guaranteed.

And if you don't have a lot of deployable assets, you should piggyback on other people or companies that do. Sometimes they don't even know they're doing the heavy lifting.

Putting My Eggs in Someone Else's Basket

When I tell people I applied the same principles to a local Easter egg hunt in South Dakota that I did twenty years later to a national sports sponsorship, I'm not just blowing smoke: Both were programs that scaled over time to provide greater value and relevance to my customers. Both piggybacked my company on existing events and took advantage of the work others were already doing.

The annual Sioux Falls Easter Egg Hunt was a small event sponsored by a large food service company that owned several pizza chains in the state. The previous year, the event had been fun but small, and I knew they wanted to get more businesses in the community involved to make it bigger. I liked the event for the goodwill it spread. It was not too commercial and had potential to reach a broad swath of my community through the children—whose parents were or potentially could be my customers. So, I decided to approach the sponsor and offer to print up some flyers and put them in stores all around town.

Was I giving the meat away? Well, this was before I met John Morrell and asked him for the free hot dogs, so I had not learned that lesson. But no, they didn't ask me for the copies. I offered. I was setting up my participation as a win-win— exposure for the event in the

| Take Control of What You Can Control |

community and broader reach for me. I saw great value for me in a donation of some time and a service that cost me pennies. I also made sure my logo was printed on all the event materials. I needed everyone to know I was involved to set up my next step: selling it myself.

I talked about the hunt in church. I talked about it in my store. I did not ask the sponsor to distribute the flyers or send them in the mail. That's broadcast. Instead, my staff and I went to every store we could. But even then we did not drop off the flyers with cashiers at local businesses and ask them to hang them up. We looked for the owner or manager—someone responsible for some decisions and sold the event to them before asking them to post the flyer. Now hundreds of people knew my business was involved in the hunt, knew what we did because I printed the flyers, and my logo was displayed in their stores around town.

By the time I was done, 400 stores had posted the flyer, up from about 10 the year before, so the main sponsor was thrilled. Next, I offered to scale up my presence and do more. Since I was already speaking about the event all over town, I offered to become the spokesperson for the group. I did interviews. I appeared on a local TV show. I went on the radio. I spoke to the Rotary Clubs and other community groups. I went out and asked for donations and prizes for the kids. I even donated some printed eggs with my logo that had candy and stickers inside so every kid got something.

By the time Easter rolled around, for the investment of time and very little money, I had become the go-to person for the event. I had piggybacked on everything and then scaled the opportunity to my company's advantage. It did not matter that the sponsoring company was much larger than my small print shop. I let them spend their zeroes while I positioned my little company as one of the big dogs.

And when the event ended and was a huge success, I stepped right in and started planning for the following year on an even larger scale: I wanted two or three TV appearances and bigger donations for bigger prizes like bicycles, and maybe I'd visit that big hot dog company and ask them for some food.

Now, contrast this with what marketing teams at big companies are doing. Let's recall the example of FedEx and its sponsorship of the PGA Tour's FedEx Cup, the yearlong men's professional golf championship. We've already cited the program as an example of how a company can creatively add and get value from its sponsorships, but it is also an eminently scalable program that could add or subtract zeroes (more or less promotion and promotional materials, more or less advertising and on-site marketing, and more or less of an online presence).

What the PGA Tour really did was offer a way to leverage a brand and create more opportunities at more PGA tournaments. Why sponsor one tournament in full when you can do a year and still have a guaranteed impact? And the PGA sees it as a win-win and has even worked with FedEx to adjust the rules to keep the playoffs fair and exciting. In fact, in working with FedEx and other companies on marketing, the PGA does a lot of the heavy lifting themselves. Just like the sponsor of the Easter egg hunt.

All businesses can and must constantly look for or create activities like these that allow them to scale up or down. Expanding your reach without bearing all the costs or responsibility is even better. Who doesn't love a piggyback ride? (Piggyback marketing is very different than a hijacking campaign in which you take over an event and turn it into your own. But that's a discussion for another time and another book.)

Remember, the goal is to take control of any physical and virtual space you can claim through the event. Look for ways to create more targeted impressions than you would get through overall sponsorship and get your audience involved. Take a page out of Big Company's book and approach the most popular local golf course and sponsor the ninth hole for a month. Then track the best scores or longest drives for a prize. Take pictures of all the participants and send them the photos. Give your audience a chance to interact and spread the word for you. Send the photos and announcements to company newsletters and all the local media you can, especially your own website or social media networks. Don't like golf? Well, then, why not try miniature golf or bowling?

The point isn't the event itself but to create something scalable and then give it legs. Whether you're running a local bicycle shop or making millions of bicycles, you cannot afford to put resources into any marketing effort, only to use it once in one medium, for one purpose. That's what the next part of scalability, the step-and-repeat principle, is all about.

Step-and-Repeat: Making Many Out of One

The concept of step-and-repeat comes from what printers call a "make ready" or the one really good copy used to make other copies. When creating marketing programs of any scale, every piece of marketing you do should be thought of as "make ready"—something that can be used over and over to create more impressions. As I said before, the definition of forward-looking is how much you can build and scale your campaign and keep doing more with what you have. Step-and-repeat gives you the best opportunity to leverage what you have by ensuring your efforts are always multiplied.

Now if you're a big company working with the PGA Tour, you have lots of zeroes to scale and step and repeat with and can build a fantasy game for consumers around the tournament, create a video game, create challenges at each course leading up to the event, and set up tents with your cameras for people to use. But you don't need zeroes for all the process; you just need to keep doing more with what you have.

Setting up a website to build a community around your event is obviously a no-brainer, but why then do you fail to update and refresh that information constantly to keep people coming back? While many businesses over-rely on social media for marketing, you'd be surprised how many businesses—even if they have a great website—also *fail* to use social media effectively or at all to step and repeat by working with other businesses that are involved, or setting up a free fan page on Facebook to post releases and updates. Encourage people to comment all the time. Amazon built an entire market around ratings, reviews, and comments fifteen years ago. You may not have millions of customers, but neither did they in 1997. Go ahead and ignore or dismiss at your peril the customer who had a negative experience and who has only twenty-five people reading her blog—there are probably twenty people just like her you are ignoring too. That's 500 people who can blog and Tweet about you to hundreds if not thousands more. It pays to be engaged.

What about video? That's something every business can and does do these days—often with a do-it-yourself feel (often because they did it them-selves or with minimal produc-tion help and some home or web-based software). Maybe the company used a local celebrity or just themselves and their kids as actors and spokespeople. Then, they buy space for these commercials on local media where you see or hear them all the time online, on the radio, and on cable and regular broadcast networks. You see them during sporting events and news programs, in the morning and late at night. At the very least, you've seen them spoofed in movies like *Old School* and *Jerry Maguire* because they are incredibly real and usually painfully funny (intentionally or not). So much so that years ago big compa-nies started looking for individuals who starred in their own videos online to work for them to capture this real appeal.

> Ask Yourself, "What Else Can I Do with This?" If the Answer Is, "Nothing," Don't Do It

But what's next? If you're taking time to make the video, think about:

- Posting the video on your internal and public web-sites, YouTube, and other social media.
- E-mailing and posting any funny outtakes too (maybe it would go viral).
- Using the video and referring to it in sales calls—maybe cutting it down and integrating small pieces into your presentations.

- Combining the video and some extra footage you shoot for no extra cost into a training video or message to your customers about specific products.
- Making an alternate or additional version of the video that promotes a contest on your website or asks viewers to text a message to your company cell phone to win a prize.

That's just a few examples for one idea to step and repeat: one step, repeated over and over. Big companies already know they need to do this. Those commercials for cars, Coke, or iPods with the music you can't get out of your head so you have to find it posted online? Super Bowl ads (before they became ridiculously expensive) that get everyone writing and blogging about the company before the event and for days after? Got Milk? Big companies and their campaigns are all about step-and-repeat. Yours should be too. And you can even make your business part of the story just like they do.

Branding Content as the New Advertising: Make Your Business the Story

First, we did TV ads. Then, TV's audience became fragmented and TiVo-ed. So, marketers shifted to product placement, which still works to an extent (*Sex and the City* did great things for Manolo Blahniks) and within certain contexts. But like I said, viewers have grown increasingly blasé about seeing their favorite actors or celebrities drinking Coke or driving Jeeps. By all means claim the spaces available—sponsor that local news program or the trivia question at the local ballpark just like the big companies do at the major league stadiums. But today, maximum impact comes from making your message an integral part of the program rather than a gimmick.

Now, by this I do not mean the hackneyed infomercials or advertorials that have been around for decades—if you want to go in that direction literally make your product or service the only story and create custom publications for your customers (as we will discuss in the next chapter). You could also produce an entire show yourself, like Donald Trump does with *Celebrity Apprentice*. Over the past few years, big companies like his have produced mini-movies, commercials, and TV/web series with A-list directors or stars or both. But assuming you do not have the zeroes to make this happen for your business, you can pursue a second option, which is harder to pitch but far less expensive and more readily scalable: Make your brand/product part of a story for the existing programs.

This is much easier to do when you're sitting in the c-suite of a hundred-year-old company with iconic status and deep pockets. I could and did get "The Donald" on the phone to pitch him for *Celebrity Apprentice*. You'd be surprised how easy it is to reach VIPs and get them to help you if you've done your homework. I got us on Trump's show by saying, "Trump…Kodak…Two great brands." Of course, like I said, it's always easier to seal the deal when the next words out of your mouth are that you're willing to spend in the high six digits. But all this is just scale. Being willing to spend a few zeroes at the local level works as well as twice that many zeroes and more at the national level. It's all about having the right scale.

What matters then is that the value you get and the value you offer is as clear as it would be if you were pitching the latest must-have technology, breakout book, or hot celebrity gossip. Forget about the big bucks involved in my last example, the important point is you need to add value to the program you are pitching in order to close the sale. No matter what medium you choose and where you start, you need to know how your value proposition fits in to make the proper pitch. For example, if you choose TV, learn:

| Think "Story" Not "Placement" |

- Who is the producer and who owns the show?
- Where does the money come from?
- Who are the hosts or actors?
- What kind of sets and segments are there?
- What kind of stories have they done recently?
- What other companies are on there?
- Who watches the show?
- Who advertises and why?

Next, determine how your brand/product will fit into the show. What do you want it to do for you? If you have products or services that the show can use in its day-to-day business like outfits for the host, go ahead and offer to provide them. If you want to strengthen your community ties, sponsor a segment honoring local heroes and charities doing good things for others.

If none of that works, come up with a story that you can play a part in. Start by thinking back to your 118—what is your hook and USP? Do you have a story or just a product? What do you have to offer—data, images, expertise—that could not be obtained from anyone else? How does your story fit into larger trends? You need to know how to take control of the pitch. Don't underestimate the desire of the person receiving your pitch to dismiss you. This is not about how great your product is or another press release, this is about ideas and perspectives—often tied to news—that go beyond your own product or business to create a story that is the vehicle for your business to get attention:

- Maybe you are doing something different to retain employees or have a plan to add more employees when everyone else is cutting—pitch a story on that.
- Maybe you are finding success with older technologies, like printing, and can show how to find value in that kind of promotion.
- Maybe you have been ripped off and now have found a way to detect counterfeits and scams that are appearing around the market.

I could go on for pages and still not cover all the possibilities. The key is integration. Don't just settle for placement or a mention for your marketing and sponsorship opportunities. Create something that is good for them and good for you and own it. That's a partnership. And if you ever forget this, try to remember this true bull story.

Not too long ago, I ran into a rancher friend of mine in South Dakota. He was having huge trouble with one of his best bulls. Now, in the ranching business, that bull is business. He needs to do his job and get those cows pregnant or the rancher can go under pretty quickly. So, the rancher called out the vet who prescribed some massive pills.

A few weeks later, I stopped by the ranch and asked how things were coming.

"I don't know," he said. "But those pills taste like strawberries."

That's my idea of a win-win: Find what's good for someone else *and* for you. No bull.

So What Does All This Mean?

Simply put, in marketing, it doesn't matter what products you build and services you offer. It doesn't matter how innovative or cutting-edge they are or if they are better mousetraps or mice. And I don't care what industry your business is in. If you don't market and sell it—if you don't get some zeroes behind it—it will fail.

Sony's Betamax is the classic marketing example: It was by most people's standards the better videotape and came out before any others, but JVC's VHS beat it out to be the industry standard through better sales and marketing tactics. VHS eventually produced economies of scale worldwide that Sony could not compete with, and Betamax was discontinued. Years later, Sony had apparently learned its lesson. When its Blu-ray (created with Philips) and the Toshiba-backed HD-DVD competed to be the industry standard, Blu-ray won not through arguing for its technical superiority but by getting Warner Brothers to drop the HD-DVD format for its movies and offer DVDs in Blu-ray only. That's the power of marketing.

Zeroes Mean So Much

A number of years ago, I was working at a company and my "buddy" was a brilliant electrical engineer who served as the chief technical officer. This guy was an engineering genius. He earned his degree at Carnegie Mellon and he eventually wound up one of the first employees at what became a major software company. No one could touch the quality of his and his team's work.

One day we were sitting in our company listening to a presentation when my buddy leaned over and said, "You know, you wouldn't have anything to do if it wasn't for me and my team. We make these great products. You couldn't do anything without what we do."

I looked at him, smiled, and said, "You know, nothing happens at all in this company unless my team sells it." You can have a great product or idea, but in the end, it means nothing unless someone sells it.

Chapter Eight

The Power of One, Part I

Speed, Relevancy, and Print

During my speeches and presentations, I often show a slide of a man standing next to a pile of envelopes that reach the top of his head. What's in the stack? A year's worth of solicitations and other mail from his bank, most of the letters addressed "Dear Occupant" and "Dear Valued Client" and "Dear Insured."

"Unacceptable," I tell the audience. They all nod—too many of them for the wrong reason. Because unlike so many other marketers, this is not when I say, "Direct mail is dead as a marketing medium" and start praising the latest social media site. If they've come to hear that, they've bought tickets to the wrong show. And so have you.

Okay, let's get this out of the way: I am a passionate promoter of the power of print. (I am, after all, writing a book.) I know to many print seems as dead as Gutenberg. But why? Of course, we need to study and master the latest ideas, technologies, social trends, and segmentations. And I try to do this every day, as you will see in the next chapter. But we can't expect *any* one medium to do the work for us. I am tired of hearing people dismiss any print as passé just because they can blast an e-mail to millions of people in a few hours or less. That's a marketing plan? That's just broadcasting with a new media mask.

It's not direct mail that's dead: Broadcast mailing *of any kind* is. That's what the slide conveys in my presentation. Of course, most people never open the "Dear Occupant" letters they get—they just throw them away. How many people call that toll-free number on the screen or reply to bulk e-mails? We're overloaded with ineffective, mindless marketing messages—marketers have just had more time to try to ruin mail and print in general as a medium.

Today, customers take a select/deselect approach to broadcasts from *every* message and medium. Sure, you must identify and attract consumers quickly and work hard to keep them. Fail to implement ongoing, proactive, cutting-edge, savvy marketing strategies that generate heavy word of mouth and sales for your company and you'll fail to stay in business. Period. But seizing consumer attention and holding it long enough to generate revenue is crucial to business success. Blasting an e-mail or text with the same lack of personalization and customization as that bank's letter is just as big a waste of time and resources.

Truth is, whether you're using postcards or posts on Facebook, it does not matter how fast your message gets there if it's irrelevant on arrival.

• Speed *and* relevancy: That's what a business needs to create pitches that get opened, read, and acted on.

Winning sales and marketing plans for smaller businesses, regardless of their budgets and scale, must also be

> **The Holy Grail of Marketing Is the One-to-One Relationship**

narrowcast, meaning absolutely relevant to the person who receives it—one person, one highly targeted, relevant message and a personalized follow-up. Remember: When communication is personalized, response rates go up *and* are faster (and cost less per lead), orders increase and revenue and profits rise—and that profitable revenue is the key to your success in marketing. How much? According to Info-Trends, personalized communications lead to increases of more than 47 percent in repeat orders, 36 percent in response rate, and 33 percent in response time alone.

That's the power of one-to-one communication or the Power of One. Your company is a mirror, and it will be tested. You reflect your customers back to themselves, showing that you see and know them. And both print and social media are effective and essential tools for accomplishing that in a customer-driven world.

To Add Zeroes, Start by Thinking, "One"

Say you own a coffee shop. Your goal is to create a place that makes you and the people you serve happy—that welcomes everyone in the neighborhood and offers a great setting with a terrific cup of coffee. That's the promise you make to your customers and to yourself as a business owner. Your obligation then is to deliver that vision to your customers through any marketing you do—in essence extending that relationship to all your communications. That's the first step in realizing the Power of One.

But customers want to think you are speaking and selling to them *alone*. They want to feel special, and businesses need to be constantly thinking about this. Think about the businesses *you* are most loyal to in your community. Chances are, the personal connection is key. Fleeting relationships are built on the failure to remember the Power of One—the power of making something relevant to a customer.

Why do you think Netflix offered $1 million to anyone who could improve the accuracy of its movie recommendation algorithm by 10 percent? Because whether you have hundreds or millions of customers, it is worth far more than that to increase the depth of your "personal" connections with those customers. You can spend all the time you want reading brand rating ratios and combing over data and audience analysis to keep up with today's multichannel, multimessage, event-driven, image-based style of marketing. You can rely on predictive marketing models. Or you can put all your marketing "eggs" in the electronic/social media basket in a vain attempt to attract customers with flash. Each of these approaches is important in its way.

But if there is a better way to grow satisfied customers than doing all you can to understand and achieve the Power of One—to gain the respect of and build relationships with your customers, avoid rejection, and close the sale to generate positive revenue—I am unaware of it. We must strive to do this on a continual basis, to use all the tools we have to keep our products and services relevant to existing and potential customers.

The question is how.

As I said before, customers and potential customers demand the same marketing promises they have always insisted on—value and relevance to their lives. Achieving the Power of One (relevant content, properly delivered, with a personalized follow-up) means using every marketing tool we have—networking, data collection and management, customer relations management, a blend of conventional and digital technologies—to create messages designed for one person that will be welcomed and read by that person.

The problem is customers these days have come to expect *much more* than just their name at the top, so to speak. We can click a button and send a sales letter—even a mail-merged one—to thousands of customers. But that does not make that communication personal or relevant.

In fact, businesses can only be sure about one thing today: Their target audiences are flooded with messages and have the ability to channel and control that flood from any medium. Consumers can select or delete at will. If they see it at all, they ask, "Is this message targeted to my interests and needs?" And they answer in about the time it takes to click a mouse or toss a letter into a wastebasket. TiVo, Do-Not-Call lists, aggressive spam filters…consumers have unprecedented strength to just say yes and no to products, services, music, web content, publications, etc.

The implications for our businesses are clear: We must cut through the clutter and assure that our messages not only reach our customers but also provide them with timely, relevant, and personalized information and offers. It's not enough to know your customers all own computers and earn $45,000 per year—you have to know what gets them interested, what attracts them to your product or service, and how to keep their attention once you've got it. The only way to make things personal in an impersonal world is through the constant building of real relationships, based on direct communication and real data and conversations. Loyalties are fleeting so we need to consistently and fiercely be sure we are connecting in the right way—the way the customer wants to stay connected.

Big businesses don't need to do that with their customers (though they are learning fast through social media). They know you'll come back if they have what you need at the price that you want. Thus, those companies are willing to deluge customers who dare order online and opt in for announcements with dozens of seemingly targeted e-mails a month

> It *Is* Personal—You Can *Never* Compete with a Big Business on Price

(check your junk mailbox). But they have no way of knowing if you bought those baby diapers for your sister's visit and would have no need for wipes for your teenage girls—even on sale. They can't know you bought the Rush Limbaugh book for your Republican friend and your bleeding blue heart can't stand to buy the Ann Coulter book the site recommends—even at 40 percent off. An almost daily blitz of computer-driven recommendations, even if based on previous ordering patterns, causes customers to tune out or opt out. There's nothing personal to their personalization. Do you think when they e-mail you they are e-mailing *you*? That a personal relationship exists? Just try to find a customer service number on those and other big business websites. The example of blind overuse of e-mailing customers sends a clear message: "I don't know who you are or what you really want, but I'm too big and important to take the time to learn. I could, but I won't."

And here's the difference: You *do* know your customers.

Say you own a neighborhood art supply store. You can study your sales receipts and see who purchased watercolor paint and who bought oil paints, who regularly buys drawing paper and who prefers arts-and-crafts supplies, and market to them as separate groups. If you own the local sub shop, you can literally separate your customers into "sub" groups—meatball, grilled chicken, veggie—and send out just the right coupon based on these preferences. Heck, you should be able to find and market to left-handed female racquetball players in central Ohio if that's your ideal customer.

Have you ever purchased something on the Internet or filled out a survey on a website and received an instant message thanking you for your order? Right then that business can offer a discount on a related product or service. What if what you purchased was something that runs on batteries or needs servicing—how about an e-mail reminder with a discount for that very product or service? Or how about a more sophisticated version of that approach, with an e-mail reminder that the battery for your digital camera needs to be replaced and by the way, we'll give you a discount on that battery. That's speaking directly to me.

What consistently surprises me is that while business owners should know this, too many remain stuck in the broadcast rather than narrowcast approach to marketing: We make our communication irrelevant when relevance is the single most important criteria influencing a consumer's decision to select or delete. We do not efficiently use all the tools available to upgrade marketing strategies and communications on a continual basis. That's the best and only way to keep products and services relevant and personal to existing and potential customers.

And a great way to start to understand what this means in more depth is through the power of print.

In the Mix of Things: Print and One-to-One Communication

A medium must be more than just innovative and exciting for its messages to cut through the clutter and drive ROI. It doesn't matter how buzzworthy the medium is if the messages are delivered ineffectively and fail to generate responses that sell your products and services. Speed and reach without relevance to the customer is meaningless. Response hinges on your messages' relevance. Relevance hinges on great communication. And great communication makes for great relationships—especially those one-to-one relationships, that holy grail of marketing. But with consumers receiving messages from so many outlets, marketers must maximize their reach by integrating several media into their marketing mix. And that's why I still love print.

Now, as I revealed earlier, I'm a print guy. From my experience in my print shop in Sioux Falls through my work today, I could detail how the digital transformation that's affected every business and communications medium has transformed print as well. Then, like experts in any business, I could rattle off lines that only make sense if you're talking to a professional in that business that just make me sound smarter than I am, like: "Just as business has been transformed by networks, data collection, and customer relations management, the print medium has been fundamentally changed by hybrid technologies combining conventional and digital printing, as well as digital workflows, variable data printing, and digital asset management systems. Presses that can print 100 percent variable data at speeds up to 1,000 feet per minute have the potential to revolutionize print media in the future."

For those of you not in the print business, "Wake up!" (Literally and figuratively.)

Media synergy is the issue, and print is a vital part of any business's communications mix. Why would you want to reject any marketing tool just because it existed when your parents started out? Reaching the consumer successfully requires more than the Internet. Besides, I'm not talking about the Yellow Pages. This is not your father's print—antiquated models that cannot hope to keep pace with the speed of today's information and the needs of today's consumers. From mass communications to mass customization, print should be an essential component in any blended media campaign and can be scaled to any budget. Print-driven, cross-media campaigns that offer high degrees of personalization—such as utilizing magazine ads or direct mail pieces that direct recipients to a landing page on the Web—are the kinds of opportunities that can achieve real results for any size business particularly small ones.

- Any medium offers creative potential if you're willing to do the work.

Now I know, some people read that and *still* dismiss me, as if integrated media campaigns that don't prioritize online strategies imply a lack of creativity—as if the mere idea of print being effective makes me a caveman (or at least stuck in the 1980s). Well, I'll take my club to the bank because print is still the biggest buy of all business marketing. According to Universal McCann, print, in one form or another, accounted for almost half of U.S. ad dollars spent in 2007. While this number will surely decline in the years to come, it is not about to be replaced by Facebook any time soon.

When it comes to reaching people across all demographics, print serves as the cornerstone of integrated communications campaigns and customer relations management (CRM)—including e-mail, Internet, SMS (texting), call centers, broadcast, face-to-face—and produces measurable, lasting results. At a time when people receive thousands of marketing messages per day from dozens of media, print's advantage comes from exactly what marketers seek: its ability to engage people on a personal level on their terms and to meet their individual needs.

Still think print is dead? Think about this the next time you sign a contract. Think about it when a child's eyes light up from a postcard from far away—and compare that to just getting an e-mail. Think about it when you get a thoughtful thank you card for your gift. Text me a thank you for my Christmas present, and I'm sure your gift will be smaller next year. We still love to see, feel, and touch things.

Remember speed and reach are meaningless without relevance to and response from the consumer. In fact, even younger people like going to the mailbox. A survey by ICOM (Information and Communications) found that 57 percent of eighteen- to thirty-four-year-olds preferred to receive product information by direct mail, as opposed to only 27 percent

Instant Isn't Everything If It Only Amounts to So Much Air

who preferred e-mail and online combined. That's a huge gap that is not going to suddenly change because of social media innovations like Twitter. Who does not like to get a printed catalog from a company they order from, even if they buy the product online? *According to comScore, consumers who received a printed catalog were twice as likely to buy something, while the Direct Marketing Association reports that 60 percent of consumer purchases are driven by printed catalogs.*

Harry Potter and the *Twilight* books proved young people still read. You think the future is going to be only texting and the Web? Research shows that electronic media are fostering the printing industry (and vice versa). Until the last recession *both* were growing and will again. And when they do, print can deliver a positive return on investment by generating quick responses and sales *and* maintaining consumer loyalty. It embodies the very essence of relevancy marketing and the Power of One.

And it only takes a little bit of knowledge to learn and apply the Power of One's key concepts in print or any medium in your marketing mix.

How to Put the Sale in the Mail

Despite what you've heard from the latest social media savant, old-fashioned mail is still the king of marketing. The Direct Marketing Association reported that U.S. advertisers spend $167 per person in direct mail to sell $2,095 worth of goods for an ROI of thirteen to one. Tens of billions of pieces of mail are sent to U.S. households every year, and more than 90 percent of that is business-to-customer mail.

Yes, mail was down during the recent recession, but find me an established marketing medium that did not experience a decline of some kind during that time. And that's still a lot of mail—all received on a one-to-one level, and unlike e-mail it cannot get spammed before it arrives. In fact, the United States Postal Service reports that 85 percent of all mail is read or visually scanned.

But does it get opened? That depends on what happens when the consumer picks it up. Most people divide mail into three piles.

- The Junk Pile: You see it and throw it away fast.
- The Get-to-It-Later Pile: Magazines, catalogs, etc.
- The Read-It-Now Pile: The personal letters, bills, and other mail you definitely read or use right away.

Getting your mail into the third pile is like hitting the marketing jackpot, but the odds are much better than the slots. As I explained at the outset of this chapter, the broadcast model of pitching—single message form letters addressed to "Dear Occupant" like the investment bank—guarantees your mail ends up in pile one even if the recipient knows you and is your customer. And with print, this is inexcusable.

The ability to personalize content is the strength of print media. Yet before I give some examples, remember what I said: Personalization only has value if the targeted individual views the communication inside as relevant to them. You know what I mean: The outside of the envelopes may address people by name but inside they are "Our Client" or "Greetings." I invest thousands of dollars with you or buy a car from you or charge all my expenses on your card and I get monthly statements with letters that say, "Dear Valued Client?" *Still?* Are you kidding me? Exactly how valuable am I?

Personalization (in print or any medium) is just the first step to alerting consumers that the information may not be a waste of their time. But personalization alone doesn't move the letter from the first to the third pile—even if it is marked "Urgent" or "Open at Once" or uses that cute handwriting font on the front to make it appear more personal than it is. Sure, it used to be that when communication was personalized, orders increased, response rates were better and faster, and overall revenue and profits rose. But the old model of personalization does not work anymore. Personalization has moved far beyond imprinting addresses on boilerplate letters that often make women Misters, ask dead men to "order now," and offer the family dog zero percent financing—preapproved!

In my big picture, personalization is just one step in seven for customizing communications in the digital age. From short runs of static content to fully automated production of personalized materials initiated by an Internet inquiry, the seven levels offer capabilities unavailable with traditional production methods, and the higher you go, the closer you are to that one-to-one relationship.

The Power of One and Printing

- **Level 1: Short runs, static content**—The same brochure for everyone.
- **Level 2: Version printing**—A common design with some unique content or language changes for specific audiences like mail going to a particular area ("Dear Neighbor"), business zone ("Dear Park Avenue Business"), or membership ("Dear Elk").

> The Key Concepts Behind the Power of One

- **Level 3: Personalized printing**—Seamlessly integrating the recipient's name and/or address into the copy ("Dear Jeff").
- **Level 4: Customized printing**—Incorporating text and images relevant to specific audiences (people who look like them or are the same age).
- **Level 5: Transactional/integrated printing**—Incorporating personalized and customized content plus "data driven" graphs and charts using information from account balances, travel histories, etc., to create highly targeted pitches.
- **Level 6: Fully customized printing**—Complex incorporation of unique text, images, and graphics like in a magazine.
- **Level 7: Automated**—Personalized/customized applications whose entire production is triggered and controlled automatically such as web request/fulfillment.

So what's that all mean?

Simple: Small businesses can build a one-to-one relationship with their customers by moving up to levels four and five and beyond. Use every tool you have (from data mining to profiling to conversations) to make your communication increasingly personal, timely, and targeted. Moving up from personalized printing to customized and transactional printing almost guarantees increased profits from repeat orders to drive overall revenue, higher response rates, faster response times, and increased order size. As the data suggests, aspiring to targeted print communications is a no-brainer: *According to a Rochester Institute of Technology survey, 67 percent of people like getting mail about new products from companies they do business with, while the United States Postal Service finds that 38 percent of households find direct mail interesting.* I'll take those odds.

Targeted Communications: Customization

Targeted print communications give businesses powerful vehicles for building relationships with prospects and customers. Knowing who your audience is, what their preferences are, understanding what and how they buy enables you to build loyalty. Target increasingly selective audiences with extremely relevant messages based on this and they will choose your offer over competing messages and media.

This is the goal of all relevancy marketing: to carry the most engaging messages to target audiences and deliver results. Targeted print simply leverages the CRM data you have now and pushes you to gather more based on responses. As your relationship grows, you can make your communications even timelier and more customized to individual preferences. And any company can do that if it is willing to put in the time and effort.

But don't just trust what I say and a bunch of numbers. Here's how some others did it by reaching level four.

Consider a bank, headquartered in New Mexico. The bank wanted to increase CD deposits and decided to offer special rates for "preferred customers." Instead of one mass (broadcast) mailing, it mined its database and broke its targets into three segments: Current

> **Not Just Personalized— Customized**

CD holders, former CD holders, and current mortgage loan customers. It then designed three sets of images and graphics that reflected the makeup of each segment: largely young (current CD holders), business professionals (former CD holders), and Hispanics (mortgage holders). Individual names and addresses were printed on every card.

The results were literally money in the bank. The campaign generated $15 million in new CD investments. According to the printer who printed the job, what surprised the bank most was how quickly people responded. Customers showed up at branch offices with the postcards in hand just two days after they were mailed.

Or take a bootmaker that wanted to create a personalized mailer to drive more traffic to a chosen retail location. Putting the customer's name on the front and in the offer was the easy part. In this case, the company created personalized maps with driving directions to the nearest retailer for each recipient. It then calculated the distance in steps. (It was selling boots remember.) So customers not only knew where they were going, they knew they were only 22,320 or 15,956 steps away from a special offer. A bar code allowed the company and the retailer to track the response rate of the mailer. The result? High double-digit response rates.

Does it cost more to do this? Yes...and no. Production costs for a customized print campaign are higher on a per-page basis but *lower* on a cost-per-response basis, and this investment usually leads to high double-digit increases in sales.

• The benefits of one-to-one campaigns in media are shifting the paradigm for cost assessment from cost per page to cost per response. This offers companies the ability to track results to a degree that's impractical or impossible with mass communications.

Want to scale it up a bit? Companies can take customization further by creating integrated personalized marketing programs that marry digital print and the power of the Web. MindFireInc did a great version of this for attendees of a conference, using a personalized matchbook (fire, get it?) with the attendees' names printed on the inside that offered a look at the hottest thing in one-to-one marketing. But the RSVP was not to a phone number, e-mail, or website. Instead, it directed them to personalized URLs (PURLs). So, if the invitation was to Debbie Smith, it directed her to respond to www.DebbieSmith.HottestThing.com

and printed the PURL on the front and back of the matchbook.

Small businesses can scale this even more by creating custom publications like the ones you see from retailers (like BJ's Wholesale and Costco), insurance companies (like Allstate), and financial services companies (like T. Rowe Price). Technology makes this affordable for as little as hundreds of copies, not hundreds of thousands. (Digital magazines are similar vehicles, but their effectiveness as a marketing tool is less established; again customization would be essential.)

These highly targeted vehicles deliver content that's relevant to narrow and well-defined audiences—namely, existing customers. This is a huge industry that turns the money that is spent on trade journal advertising, PR to get editorial content in certain pubs, and inserts in other media and uses it to develop and implement a company's own magazine. The advantages, especially if you offer good content (not just infomercials) is that you control the ads, the editorial, and the messaging to a specific target audience. There are more than 100,000 different custom publications produced annually in North America, many of them producing targeted offers to their customers—a magazine just for them.

That's the essence of what customization offers businesses: personalization that feels like it was meant for its customers. Isn't that all anyone wants when they walk into a coffee shop or store, get a phone call, open a piece of mail or e-mail? That's how you get out of the first pile and into the second and third pile of mail.

Now, consider what you could do if you were already *in* the third pile of mail.

Targeted Communications: The Transpromo Experience

Every communication we have with a customer—heck, *anyone* but let's stick with customers right now—is an opportunity to sell something. If you are just transmitting information and not using it in any way to offer more, you've missed an opportunity. Remember: Marketing is about selling a product, and if that product and your company is part of a customer's life in the smallest way, well, then, you have an opportunity to keep connecting and building your brand with them one-to-one.

That's what transpromo marketing means.

Transpromo was actually a term that I started using when I was working with a digital printer. It means using transactional statements in a promotional way, marrying pieces of paper and the digital statements everyone has to read or scan (telephone, credit card, utility bills, airline miles) with highly personalized advertising and offers that present the ultimate ability to reach the one-to-one level.

Hundreds of millions of transactional statements are mailed (or e-mailed) every month like clockwork: how much money we owe, how many minutes we've used, how many miles or points we have. If companies have this information, they can use it to select and place relevant ads right on the statement. Not on those little pieces of paper that come in the envelope, but right on the front of the statement where the customer sees it. The "real estate" is there. The statement is already going

> **Transpromo Turns the Mundane into Money**

to the customer and landing in that third pile. For the business sending the statement, transpromo can turn a cost center—the billing statement, which costs money to create and mail out—into a profit center.

If you're handling marketing for a car company, you know exactly what kind of car each of your customers drive, how old they are, where they live or work, and more. Instead of a text-only billing statement or putting the same picture of the same car on every statement, you can place a picture of each customer's car right on the statement. For example, I live on the prairie in South Dakota. I need and use a truck. My truck should not only be on the statement but pictured on a dusty road. Next to that, you can have tailored, highly relevant ads offering me accessories that would appeal to someone like me—my age, my gender, my specific zip code, my income. Today's data mining technologies make all of this possible and affordable.

If you're managing marketing for a phone company, you already know what model phone most of your customers use, their ages, and other demographic information. Instead of sending out a bill that simply lists the charges for each family member's phone, you put pictures of each one's phone next to his or her charges, along with ads for accessories tailor-made for those phones. For example, next to the picture of Dad's phone you might place an ad for a belt clip, while next to the picture of the daughter's phone you can put an ad for ring tones a girl her age must have.

If you don't send out bills or other transactional statements, you can create mail that your customers "must" open, which gives you a chance to use transpromo techniques and improve your bottom line. Many stores track birthday information, offering a $10 "reward"—knowing full well that any customer's average purchase is about $50. A small business could offer a "gift" coupon inside a handwritten birthday card, not a simple "$10 off" but "$10 off your next purchase of $50 or more."

When customers see that you're giving them relevant offers backed by good incentives, and not just taking space in their recycling bins with ads they can't throw out fast enough, customer retention and response will improve. InfoTrends reported that 63 percent of consumers preferred a personalized statement that contained relevant offers within their statement to advertising inserts. Recognizing this, some companies have started charging partners fees to put promotional offers on their statements. Why not? With an advanced ability to mine their data and provide relevant offers, it is well worth the investment.

A large bank and a luxury watch company in Europe mined transaction data and used transpromo to produce a 65 percent response rate. They simply placed targeted promotional material to top prospects in envelopes mailed by the bank. The watch offer went to prospects who spent more than 5,000 euros per month and who also spent more than 5,000 euros per year on jewelry.

That's all it took for a 65 percent response rate. That's the power of transpromo and reaching level five. As marketing increasingly moves from reaching many consumers at the same time with the same message (broadcast) to communicating with each person on a one-to-one basis (narrowcast), applications such as personalization and transpromo give print a distinct advantage in helping keep businesses closely connected with their customers. And any business can get there—and must, because customers demand it. They do it every day with the information they receive on the Web through RSS feeds and blog aggregators. You need to do it with what you send them too.

So, small businesses have a choice: Produce more customized products and target the individual or offer fewer customized products and be more mass. I like being and feeling like an individual, but that does not mean I want to live alone on a pond like Thoreau. I like the idea of waking up in a day when the best parts of the customer experience are like that in *Minority Report*—where a scan of my eye shows me what I've bought before and what I might like now. It's not an invasion of privacy. It's not Big Brother. It's information targeted to me *and* for me. That's empowering. That's the Power of One.

So What Does All This Mean? Jeff Wants Me to Stop E-mailing and Kill a Tree? How 1975

These days any brand (digital or otherwise) must get its products and services to market faster than its competitors and make sure that what it does makes a difference in the lives and businesses of its customers. The emerging communications environment requires businesses to be quick, nimble, innovative, technologically savvy, and ready to harness the resources and tools it has to build its brand. But digital does not mean electronic alone. Businesses can still use print as part of the blend for its effectiveness in reaching people on a personal level.

That's a mouthful, I know (especially after the crash course I gave you in this chapter), but that's the core of what I call the "Power of Printing"—its ability to help deliver the Power of One as part of the marketing mix for a business.

So, when I was invited to give a presentation called "The Power of Printing," I was delighted to sign on. Note the title of the speech—their choice not mine. Not the power of social media, but the power of print. If the people who hired me had asked me to speak about social media, I would have. Anyone who knows me knows I am a huge print *and* social media advocate. I've even been called a social media "darling." Call it cognitive dissonance if you want, but I prefer to keep all my options in play.

As so often happens, one of the attendees missed the wording on the invitation, the sign outside the ballroom, the title slide, the handout, and every word I said. He wanted the social media talk I was not asked to give. He heard what he heard and then decided to "report" back to his "online community" that I was a dinosaur about to drive my company into the ground. Print? Hah!

And that's the power of social media—anyone can have a platform and say anything they want. That includes me. So, before I Tweeted and posted and blogged to the tens of thousands of people I connect with regularly online about what I really said, I wrote that guy a personal note and dropped it in the mail. I wanted to make sure he paid attention to my Power of One.

The Power of One, Part II

Marketing and Networking in the Age of Social Media

All my life, I have sold something. As a kid, I sold subscriptions to *True Grit*, a national boy's life magazine. Every year, I won the Little League baseball barbecue ticket-selling contest by selling tickets to everyone in my neighborhood and the neighborhoods next to mine. When I was thirteen, I started a lawn mowing business to buy the Schwinn I wanted. And as a teenager trying to make some real money, I sold Amway products.

Today, Amway is one of the largest private companies in the world, specializing in health and personal care products. And it still follows the same direct-selling, multilevel marketing model it did when I started: trained sales representatives setting up parties or going door-to-door to pitch those products. Even back then, I knew my strengths. With dreams of a six-figure payday, I put on my white shirt and black tie and headed out to the nicest homes to sell them one-to-one Amway's laundry detergent.

As I headed up the path of the first house, I had my

pitch down cold: Amway would make those whites whiter and brights brighter than any other detergent. This was exactly what I told the woman behind the screen door, but she remained unconvinced, devoted as she was to her current brand. I refused to back down.

I was just about to push harder when it happened: A huge bird pooped on my shoulder and it immediately started to run down the front of my shirt.

"You know," she said. "A little Tide will get that out."

Now imagine the same scene, only there are thousands upon thousands of people ready to either poop on or praise your pitch, your company, and you. That's what social media offers: the potential to win or lose at a speed and scale that seemed impossible a generation ago. Today, millions in your budget is nice, but you don't need that much to get noticed if you take the time to use online/social media effectively to build, network, promote, and sell your business. The question is, "How?"

Even if you don't want to join the social networking world—even if you'd rather only read magazines—you still have a responsibility to stay on top of it for your business. You may not want to know that your friend is getting her toenails painted or your customer is cleaning up baby vomit, but many people do—more than a third of the country visit social media networks of some kind. And those same people just might be saying something about you and your business.

I know, the chatter is deafening and constant but keeping up with that chatter, positive or negative or neutral, is a direct line to the Power of One. Social media is an essential part of a well-diversified multimedia marketing campaign. Businesses have already used social media like

Twitter to get instant feedback or make sure their customers know about special deals, events, or just where to find their mobile service on a given day—information given directly to those customers on their phones and PDAs. Your customers are talking to each other "out there" and you can forge real one-to-one connections with them. So much so that the measurement of those connections is in hearts and minds (relationships) not eyes and ears (impressions). No business can miss out on that.

• Social media is not exercise: You should not do it moderately. You need to drive it, set the tone, and support it or it will cost you more than money.

A small business can and must use social networking sites and tools to increase its ability to sell itself. They have changed the face of marketing. The problem is social media has made too many businesses and marketers sloppy and invited a lot of bad behavior that threatens it as an effective tool. You can't expect impersonal, unsolicited blast e-mails and impersonal posts to achieve the Power of One. That's just Vi@gr@. In other words, junk.

Facebook, Google, LinkedIn, Plaxo, Twitter, YouTube, RSS, SEO, StumbleUpon, BearShare, Pandora...a website is not enough to do business these days. I cannot tell you *what* media and approach will be most effective for your business. (Heck, by the time you read this, some of the sites I just mentioned

> Having a Blast? Stop

will likely be gone or replaced with the latest hot technology, and millions of new groups will have formed within and outside these sites.) I can tell you that involvement in social media will grow your brand, strengthen the connection between you and your company's key audiences, and keep you grounded and aware of what's really happening with your business.

And before you start, I can also tell you this: Regardless of what the service is called, understanding and using social media the right way is of vital importance to your Power of One. It's well worth the time investment to do it right and win before you begin.

First... Do You Speak Klingon?

Let's start by calling social media what it really is: a fast, electronic version of groups like the Chambers of Commerce, Rotary Clubs, trade associations, or school and fan clubs. Social media is not new, the *technology* is. Word of mouth is still word of mouth; networking is still networking. Hardware store owners, coin collectors, Deadheads, Trekkies, kids who want to play chess — people with similar interests have always found a way to connect using whatever media or space was available to them.

The difference is that the Internet and social media sites allow the kids who dressed like Klingons from *Star Trek* to *avoid* the kids who beat up the kids who dressed like Klingons and meet, share, and connect directly and at warp speed with all those people without ever leaving the house. And just like the off-line groups of yore, when one group gets too big or fractures from competitive interests, new

> Not Community,
> *Communities*

194

microgroups form. That's why you see niche social sites spring up (some with millions of members) when sites like Facebook get too big to represent specific groups' interests.

With social media we are not talking about community but *communities*—millions of individuals divided into countless shared interest groups, each one of them constantly looking for people, information, products, and services they like or dislike online. As a result, messages reach these people and groups faster too, and can spread or disappear just as quickly.

• To make sure your messages have a chance of getting through and are relevant and well received, don't think about social media as one big conversation to sell into. Rather, they are many different conversations with those communities where relationships matter before the sale.

Otherwise, you're just speaking Greek (or Klingon) to all of them.

Social Media Is a Conversation with Communities

People often ask me, with everything that business owners and executives have to do in a given day, why I (an avowed print man) take the time to use social media to the extent that I do and why I strongly recommend others do the same. My first reason is simple—there's no better way to engage the various communities that are important in my professional and personal life.

To be honest, I first started using social media to enable

my family to keep in touch with me while I traveled for work. But I soon realized the benefits of updating my fellow employees, our customers, the press and bloggers, and anyone else who wants to keep updated on what's happening with my life and business. Of course, I have always engaged in conversations with my family and friends, customers, and employees, but now I have direct, unfiltered links to thousands of them.

Once I started reaching out and responding to all these different groups of people, I found social media to be a really easy (and addictive) way to inform and educate them about my business's activities. To make sure the right audiences see any targeted messages, I often tag my updates to identify them as marketing or business related. But even for the business stuff, most people are really excited to learn what is happening, right as it happens. It gives people an inside look at activities I'm involved in.

For me, it could get pretty glamorous—the Academy Awards, PGA Tour Golf Tournaments, *Celebrity Apprentice*—and I gave followers of these experiences an inside look and a chance to share in the excitement. But your experiences don't have to be close to this big to attract and captivate your followers. No matter who you are, the Oscars only happen once a year. What fills the space between? What's going on in the kitchen of your restaurant? What is under the hood of that car? What's getting delivered today? The key is conveying everything with passion for what you do (I love my job!) as you're doing it (I love what I'm doing!)—and maintaining that

Connections Come from the Momentous and the Monotonous

commitment and connection to your communities with regular updates.

But I have to be careful to keep my feeds and posts as balanced as possible. They can't be too commercial. So, while I might Tweet about the hot new product we have, I also Tweet about my weekend hunting trips or my favorite places to eat (and if you have seen me, you know I like to eat). I even try to add a bit of humor. After all, there is no need to be serious or selling all the time.

The goal is to be accessible and real. That's why I sometimes respond to customer queries myself and why I weave personal activities into my updates—I want my personality and thus the personality of my business to come through. That's also why I do my own posts—you can't fake it with social media. No matter where I work, I will always be me: a guy from South Dakota with a cool job he loves who can't help getting excited at some of the great things his company does. This is not self-promotion.

• The goal of all my social media activities is to build my company's brand organically through my activities by maintaining my business's relevance and keeping it top-of-mind.

Despite the immense responsibility this requires, I find it *exciting*. And so should you. There's no better feeling than to get a response to a post from a customer about something they didn't know we did or to hear about their support of our activities. And I'm selling all the time too. It doesn't matter to me if I'm selling one product at a time or a million. Any time a customer writes me with a problem, I try to help. I got someone to buy a camera yesterday—that's still effective.

Of course, that's not to say you won't get pooped on. Social media can be your friend when you succeed, but it can be your enemy when millions with a few clicks can see your embarrassments, missteps, and mistakes. And you will receive comments about your products and services both good and bad. But that's a benefit! Receiving negative comments directly—not filtered through people whose job it is to manage negative feedback—gives you an unvarnished truth that can only help you better define and address issues and help you understand what's happening in real time to you and your company's products.

Sure, openness sucks sometimes, but social media has put the customer in charge—it has served up the Power of One before you even sit down. And that's not changing any time soon.

You May Not Think Customers Are Always Right, but Now They Are Always in Charge

Forrester Research calls social media the final push in the movement from "top-down" to "bottom-up" innovation in business. I could not agree more. Traditionally, inspiration came from the executive level, now it is customer driven:

- Observing customer needs now drives marketing innovation.
- Structured, one-way broadcasts are dead—spontaneity and what Forrester calls "controlled chaos" are in.

- Social media, e-mail, and intranets are the primary tools with the traditional surveys, focus groups, and storyboards of yore taking a secondary role.

These points are also echoed in "Fluent: The Razorfish Social Influence Marketing Report" (http://fluent.razorfish .com/publication/)—a must-read for marketers on the power of social media, detailing the end of top-down approaches, the importance of socializing with customers, and the need for authenticity.

What does all this mean? As Walt Mossberg and Kara Swisher of the *Wall Street Journal* said, this is now Web 3.0; information can be delivered and feedback can happen from any device, almost anywhere and at any time. Small and medium-sized businesses should note that many big companies—even those that fail on e-mail—have figured this out quickly and as a result

> **Conversations Are About Talking *and* Listening and Then *Acting***

completely changed their perception of feedback and how to act on it. Companies like IBM now make social media an essential component of any well-blended marketing campaign. Companies like AT&T use social media to expand collaboration across groups both inside and outside the business. Companies like Wal-Mart use social media to give honest user reviews, negative or positive, of products from their buyers and managers and then allow customers and vendors to respond. Smart companies even change products based on social media feedback (for example, adding or subtracting features of a product because consumers blogged about it and said they would like that feature).

Wait, did I say big companies *want* to hear the whines and moans and everything else that's going on out there and then be responsive to and engage it? Absolutely. But they are still big companies. All this entrepreneurial spirit, spontaneity, controlled chaos, and relationship building is nothing new to small businesses. They are playing on your ball field—so get in there! You could never match their media buys, but in social media, scale and speed are available to all businesses—start acting "small" and you can capture a global audience.

The goal is to get people to talk about you—whether good or bad. The worst thing that can happen is that people say nothing about you. Start friending people and other businesses and linking to them off your social media sites to build your network; participate on other sites and they will start to reciprocate. Don't expect anything to happen overnight (this is a grassroots approach), but the conversations are out there, so get in on them and then initiate and stay in on others. As the *New York Times* reported, smart public relations and marketing professionals, especially those working with online brands and start-ups, have already seized the change and now "must know hundreds of writers, bloggers, and Twitter users instead of having six top reporters on speed dial."

Most businesses don't need some high-priced consultant to get started. Mitch Joel's excellent book *Six Pixels of Separation* offers a terrific education about how the Internet has dramatically changed the way you do business and shows how anyone can improve their business outreach by following some simple and straightforward techniques.

And just remember my four social media Es for customer relations: engage, educate, excite, and evangelize.

Engage

Remember the guy who wanted me to speak about social media during a speech about print? Social media gives him a powerful platform to preach from—it gives *everyone* a potentially powerful platform, and each person is connected to other people who could be your customers, so be prepared to engage them all. And engagement means actually *engaging*—regularly.

> **The Four Es: Engage, Educate, Excite, Evangelize**

Behind my desk, I have three screens devoted to me and my company's online activities, giving me "eyes" on my posts and the responses and searching for all the posts and news about my company and the competition. (You think this is just about *you*?) It's kind of like air traffic control, and there are plenty of aggregators and consolidators that can make this process as efficient as possible and even help generate followers or traffic to your site and blog, such as TweetDeck, Seesmic, or StumbleUpon. My social media connections are so vast, I need a team to maintain my three blogs, two Facebook pages, multiple Twitter accounts, ongoing podcasts, YouTube posts, and more.

But regardless of your company's size, the more you do, the bigger your responsibility to engage. Of the four Es, none of the others matter without this one. Every day, you must go to the screens, find out what people are saying about you, engage them, and find others to engage you. Speed is your friend, and time is your enemy in social media, and things multiply fast. If it is good, you must respond quickly to make sure that good feeling can multiply. If it is bad, you've got to find the people who hate you, talk to them, and cool the problem down fast so it doesn't escalate. Assuming the people pooping on you are real with genuine problems and not shills or spies for the competition, the engagement always leads to a chance to educate and create new relationships. The more you lead, the more they will follow.

Educate

In marketing, there is something called the "Rule of Thirds." For every marketing program or initiative you launch:

- A third of the people will get it immediately.
- A third of the people will get it eventually.
- A third of the people will never get it.

In the old marketing models, you never worried too much about the last third—you just told people what you had and what it was about. In the age of social media, you have a responsibility to engage and at least try to educate all of them. Ignoring them no longer means they ignore you, and they can find people to join their "team" faster than you can hit delete. And you need to educate them politely.

People who work for me sometimes tell me that when a person says something negative to me face-to-face I have a tendency to respond inappropriately with, "Bite me." They tell me I'm being impolite. So, I say, "Bite me, please." That's sort of what you do with the third that never gets it online. You grow a thick skin—there's no crying in social media—and say, "Sorry that you feel that way, perhaps you might be interested in the competition's services. Here's a link."

But what really jazzes me is when the customers who do get it have a problem with something you do or sell. The ability to educate your customers in real time why your product is better or excelling and what the benefits are is incredible. And if you are wrong and changes need to be made, you can tell your customers quickly and directly what you are going to do about the problem. Sure, maybe some people remain dissatisfied or just want to bitch unconstructively, so I go back to what I said before, thank them, and maybe point them to a competitor. But if I can solve a person's problem, then we both get excited about the process and the relationship. I've educated and excited at the same time, and now I can get them to evangelize about what happened. That's the wow factor for me: getting millions of people to talk about your business from a simple dedication to one-to-one education in social media.

Excite

Once you have engaged and educated your customers, you need to generate some kind of excitement to keep the majority of them coming back and sharing what you do with more of their connections and communities. Whether a contest, a challenge, or just a chance to be a part of something, the more you give them a reason to keep coming back, the deeper the relationships. Remember when M&M's let their customers choose the new color? The response was tremendous and that was pre–social media. Imagine how big the debate would be today—all perfectly on message!

Remember, excitement is not only about engaging your customers but your whole community including your employees—it lifts the mood of the company as a whole. Not everyone can work on that cool product or attend the big event, but everyone can feel connected to it. It is like great packaging for what lies inside—you can't have a cool product with crappy packaging and lousy messaging. Social media is a conduit for energy and excitement and allows you to rally your communities around what you are doing and extract more from those communities.

Evangelize

And once you have your communities engaged, educated, and excited, help them be your brand ambassadors. What your company is doing won't matter a lick if more and more people don't know about it, and no business can spread the word on its own. It needs evangelists.

Sometimes we overestimate the impact of comments on the Internet: A few positive comments can make us celebrate too soon, and a few negative comments can throw us into a tailspin. But when those comments come from your evangelists, the impact cannot be understated: Evangelists create scale and are the happiest result of a business doing the first three Es right.

Some people call it word-of-mouth advertising. Malcolm Gladwell's *The Tipping Point* became a huge best seller exploring this idea. Social media just makes the message spread faster than ever before. So, engage and make great impressions with your most active ambassadors through your education and excitement, and your message will reach millions instantly. They will create social media reverberation for what you do and say by taking your message and sending it out to their followers, friends, BFFs, etc. Not only will they post about you positively but they will "go off" on unfair and negative criticism on your behalf—something you can't do on your own without revealing your self-interest.

ROI (Return on Investment) Versus ROI (Return on Ignoring)

Okay, so social networking drives value for people and businesses by:

- Connecting us in new ways.
- Reconnecting us to things we miss or want.
- Helping us achieve or experience new things and in new ways.
- Allowing us to find others like us with speed and scale.
- Keeping us engaged with our communities.

But what about definitive ROI (return on investment)?

Well, it's not hard to compare "before and after" and recognize the difference that social media can make. The intangible and anecdotal results are in—it's a valuable way to support and grow the brand and an invaluable way to maintain a dialogue with consumers.

> **Measuring the Return**

205

Given the low costs and barriers to entry, even the smallest businesses can see very tangible returns from its participation in social media from increased customer consideration to sales leads to direct product purchases. In addition, I'm a process person who likes to do one thing and then repeat it many times. Social networking allows me to leverage my activity in all parts of my business on- and off-line. That can be as simple as having Twitter feed into my Facebook or making sure press releases get used across all media.

"Fair enough," you might say. "But what about those zeroes?"

That's more elusive. The cost to your business is mostly in the time it takes to manage social media. At a small business, that responsibility usually falls on you or your partner, someone who works for you, or maybe a spouse, friend, or colleague—and those people have other full-time jobs. Even at larger companies, the people handling social media are often connected to other divisions or content management for the company's websites. (It wasn't until 2008 that a big company hired a chief blogger.) Moreover, all of this happens on-and-off twenty-four hours a day. So, it can be hard to precisely quantify traditional ROI, because the time spent is hard to track.

In the absence of hard numbers, I like to talk about a different ROI: the return on ignoring. I think this is just as important as traditional ROI. If you're not engaged then you're missing out. Like I said, conversations are going on with or without you, and the worst thing that happens is...nothing. So,

- Overcome the challenges and capitalize on the opportunities;

- Set a policy for engagement and the other Es;
- Decide who speaks for you, and make sure you and whoever else is handling your social media engagement speak with one voice; and
- Get out there and establish and protect your brand.

And remember: quality over quantity. I may be one of the top Twitterers in the executive or c-suite level, but my Tweets barely reach 10 percent of the top Twitterers overall. Your customers may expect a constant stream of information from you to stay engaged, but the number of impressions you make has to take a backseat to the value and impact each post makes.

If you can remember only two things about engagement and ROI, have it be, "Quality leads to impact." And don't be a Twanker.

Why Twankers Use Vi@gr@ — the Importance of Being a Good Steward

Impersonal or unsolicited blasts or responses like those solicitations for Vi@gr@ and "Rolexes" have ruined e-mail. Opt-in newsletters can be better than e-mails, but only if they actually have news to offer and something customized for me. Without personalization, they too will lose their effectiveness over time — a short time. Mobile messaging? The first time you send me an unsolicited text I'm throwing my phone through the window.

Simply put, I have no tolerance for people who use any kind of electronic media in bad form or are rude — something I tend to be direct about when confronted with it, no matter what the form, online or face-to-face.

But I reserve a special contempt for people who abuse social media. That's how marketing media can get destroyed—by the businesses, large and small, who deluge us with countless impersonal solicitations and try to exploit it as part of their marketing mix, not to mention the spammers and scammers looking for a quick buck. We must be good stewards and use our technology tools wisely. And to show you how far I'm willing to go, I even invented a new term for the people who misuse Twitter. Here's how it happened.

I was invited in July 2009 to deliver the keynote at Twitter's 140 Characters Conference in New York City. (As you probably know, Twitter's social networking or microblogging site allows users to send people who follow them text-based updates—or Tweets—of 140 characters or fewer that can include video or other links.) At that point, I just looked old enough to be the father of the really smart, cool, and young crowd I was about to present to. But by the time I was done, I was the father of a term none of them could forget.

My keynote was on corporate leadership in the social networking scene. As I spoke, I found myself looking for a name for those people who microblog in bad form or are rude—a perfect moment for some "crowdsourcing." Crowdsourcing is essentially making an open call to a group of people rather than assigning the task to one person or a small team behind closed doors. Before social media, you needed a captive audience to crowdsource, and that day I had both.

Who better to find that name than the "Twitterati" in attendance or watching online—surely they were among the biggest Tweeters of all and definitely "characters" in their own right. So, with my South Dakota directness, I challenged those in the audi-

Don't Be a Twanker

ence and those following in the Twittering world to identify the kinds of people abusing the service, make a list
of their transgressions, and give them a name right there.
The resounding response from the crowd led to—drum
roll please—Twanker. A new word was born—certainly
suitable for microbloggers and now you, too.

Twanker (noun)
   1. A person, organization, or company who
   uses bad form or exhibits bad behavior on Twitter
   ("His constant posting of misinformed and mean-
   spirited Tweets resulted in the group labeling him a
   Twanker.")

To the delight of the crowd, I started to rattle off some
Twankers like the person who autoresponded when I
agreed to follow him, "Thanks for the tweet! Would you
work an hour per day, to make $5,000/month? If so, go
here…"—talk about "lose before you begin!" Upon hearing each transgression, the audience responded by shout-
ing, "You are a Twanker!"
   Following are the types of Twankers I identified that
day at the conference (adapted here for a broader marketing and social media perspective). I'm sure there are more
Twankers out there. That is the cool thing about crowdsourcing in the age of social media; it's always changing
and building and evolving in good and bad ways. But the
more things change—Twankers like these have always
existed in marketing—they just move faster online. Watch

out for them and understand how to respond to them, but most importantly: *Don't be one of them!*

Twankers are not just rude, they undermine your efforts to achieve the Power of One.

Hijackers

The least genuine people, they hide their true reason for being out there. At an event or conversation online, they are representatives of the competition but do *not* disclose their affiliation and proceed to badmouth your company, your products or services, and you. In politics, these tactics have led to strict marketing rules and an entire "truth in media" industry. But those rules do not always apply in business marketing—honesty is often self-imposed. Sometimes these people are discovered—Twitterers and other microbloggers pride themselves on exposing undisclosed bias, often requesting an apology from the offenders or asking them to move on. Most people will, but only after they are discovered. Bad form. Rude. Go find your own event, and please tell the truth. You are a Twanker!

Ambushers

These people come out of nowhere. They just jump in and start ranting about one thing or another, often using foul language. Someone once sent me a Tweet to tell my company and me to get out of business and go away in especially offensive terms. Dude, that is out of line. My mom reads those posts, you Twanker.

Lazy Autorepliers

Twitterers know it's proper etiquette to follow those who follow you. You don't have to but it's polite. What I find interesting is when I click to follow a person who first follows me and I get the following message: "Thanks for following me, I hope to reciprocate and follow you soon as I can get to it. I am so busy responding to the thousands who want _____." Um, forgive me, but you started this by following me first. I was being polite by responding. It's not the best way to start off our new relationship, especially if you are representing your business. You, sir, are a Twanker!

Tweeting Terrorists

These people take a product, a comment, or a company and then maliciously create some kind of controversy out of it (stirring the hornet's nest so to speak) before backing away to watch what happens. Then, they pop back up a few days later to let you know they are a social media consultant or some other type of potential vendor and they can help solve the problem. Frankly, we didn't have one until you artificially started one. Now take your fake white horse and go away, Twanker.

Fake Followers

Twitter asks you to answer one question with your posts: "What am I doing?" Recently a reporter for a major newspaper was following Sir Richard Branson and me, and in her story wrote how she didn't really care about some of the meetings we were Tweeting about like the meeting I had with a marketing team in Brussels. Well, I did not ask her to follow me. She signed up for it. My response? "If you don't like what I do, then quit following me!" Don't judge me. I am grateful for people who follow me, but don't criticize me just because you don't like what I say or the activities I do, just go away. I have immense respect for constructive criticism and debate, but that was not what she did. Ma'am, you are a Twanker!

Hawkers

These people don't really want to be in a conversation with you; they are just screaming to the world that they have something to sell, like a slicked up barker at a carnival. It might work there but not here. And don't ask me to re-Tweet your hawking tweets. If we find them interesting, funny, or educating, we will. Promise. That's what social media is all about, Twankers!

Like I said, there are probably more examples. And if you object to my names or suggestions, that's okay; healthy debate is a good thing. Just don't be a Twanker about it. That will destroy a good thing and the real appeal of ˙social media: its ability to narrowcast. I have always relied heavily on word of mouth, the most effective form of marketing and advertising. In the past, the best way of generating that was to talk up my business at meetings and events, place ads, post billboards, and hand out or mail out brochures and flyers. Today, social networking sites allow me to join or initiate thousands of conversations without delay, making all my other media buys that much more effective.

Social media helps start relationships immediately—not just the *illusion* of a relationship but a relationship that looks and feels real. That's why you need to keep using, innovating with, and being a good steward of all our marketing tools but especially social media because it is built on the very essence of the Power of One. It forces you to be compelling, to share and have conversations. It allows you to engage and be a part of your customers' worlds from the very start, making your products or services as relevant as possible to your customers' worlds on a one-to-one basis.

What Goes Around...

When I was seventeen, I lived with my dad and step-mother on an Air Force base in Rapid City, South Dakota. I had just finished some yard work late in the afternoon, set the sprinkler for the lawn and flowers, and walked inside when my stepmom walked groggily into the living room. She was a nurse and worked night shifts, so she slept during the day and had not heard me come inside. Just then, the sprinkler made its pass across the front of the house. With a loud "Swoosh!" it spread water across the living room window, startling her.

"My gosh! Did you see that?" she exclaimed. "Where did that rain come from and so hard and fast!"

My dad and I chuckled.

"Yeah, it was something," I said quickly. "But just wait, it'll come again."

Whoosh!

"How did you know that?" she gasped before the third pass came and we started laughing as she chased me out of the room.

So it is with social media and will be again with the next "big thing" in marketing. Hard and fast, it too shall come again, startling us with its power and speed and forcing us to mistake it for something it can never be: the be all, end all. The latest marketing tools are all like the gold rush to me—only the people who sell the "shovels" make guaranteed money. The rest are just mining with everyone else as fast as they can, staking claims and trying to strike it rich. And like those gold prospectors, the pursuit can consume and destroy you by distracting you from everything else that matters.

That's why I look for balance—in my businesses and in all I do but especially in marketing. As a small business owner, I can't afford to ride initial waves of speculation in hot innovations like social media, especially if it means ignoring all the other tools in my marketing toolbox. I need to take my time and learn what it is; what I can expect from it and what it expects from me; when and how it will deliver for my business. Otherwise, I will get too caught up in the hype and get lost just like the people who rushed into print, radio, TV, direct mail, the Web, and all the marketing media that came before. But I also can't afford to wait too long.

> ### Use a Tool, Don't Be One—Be Prudent

What's next? Who knows? But like that sprinkler you can be sure something is going to make a splash, and you need to stay on top of the social evolution and technological advances that repeatedly transform what your customers expect and how you reach them.

That's how it must be in social media and *all* marketing these days, but psst...want to know a secret? That's how it has always been in small business.

The speed you need, the tools you have, and the competition you face have all changed, but you must constantly remind yourself that the basic principles of running a business—who you are and what you stand for—have *not* changed. The mirror has always tested us on three words: community, authenticity, and honesty. Your marketing will and should reflect the personality of your company, and if you are not genuine, you won't last very long. Anyone who says otherwise is just trying to sell you something.

Conclusion

Sell! Sell! Sell! Sell Everything You Can! Even If It's You... Just Sell!

JEFFREY HAYZLETT IS ALL THE RAGE ONLINE, BUT IS HE PROMOTING MORE THAN HIMSELF?

Sometimes I hate headlines. This particular one was the headline for a Forbes.com interview about my work, and it felt familiar. The media, bloggers, vloggers, and beyond have dubbed me the "Celebrity CMO" for my TV and social media work, my appearances at events around the world, and my quotes in all kinds of publications on the latest business and marketing news. But people throughout my career have constantly noted how I seem to be selling myself in what I do, because, well...I am. Should someone else? I've always felt the need and obligation to be "out there." That's my job no matter how many zeroes the company has in the bank: to get exposure for the brand.

This particular interviewer got it right. Despite the provocative headline, the article concluded that I promote myself...but not at the expense of the company. Because from every hand I shake to every Tweet I make, I am *always* selling my company. That's what I was hired to do. So, when someone says, "Jeff, you're promoting yourself," I reply, "You're right. Every time I promote myself, I promote the company. I'm living the brand." My company, my customers, my community, my employees, the media, and my family know my MO, and I want you to know it too: Sell you; sell the company.

I don't exist *separately* from my company—I am the company. I put my personality into every company I own or work for and am its unabashed ambassador. I see myself as an asset—the ultimate tool in my toolbox. I'll do almost anything—and seemingly have—to get attention. If I can be a conduit for that attention, bring it on. I love what I do whenever and wherever I am doing it. Every company I have owned or worked for becomes my favorite thing or I wouldn't be doing it.

Even my clothes reflect the company I work for. I am forever wearing my companies' logos in family photos. You could trace my loyalties through the shirts and colors I'm wearing—so much so my wife has implemented logo-free dinner nights. Seriously. She says, "We are going out to dinner, and you cannot wear anything with a logo." But I'm so immersed in what I do, I feel naked without my logos. When I look in the mirror, I like to be reminded that I am my company. Plus I'm a big guy. I know I'm a walking billboard that draws attention. Do you really think I wore a tux with a bright yellow vest to the Oscars as a fashion statement? Well, *Project Runway*'s Tim Gunn did. He thought I looked "smashing" and asked why I chose to wear it. And I, of course, told him it was my company's color and got to work my company's name in for free.

Simply put, I sell what I do through everything I do.

That's a huge part of how I breathe life into my work and businesses and *keep* them breathing: I don't just sell "it." I believe in it—I live it and love it. That's how you win, and I want to win. I want to win every single time no matter what I am doing, whether it is in sports, a game night with friends, or in business. My wife used to say to

> **Feel Alive from the Work You Do and Win**

my son and daughter when they ran off to play a game, "Have fun!" I yelled, "Have fun and *win!*"

That's what I do every day. But I can't win—I can't succeed—if my company loses in the process. To the untrained eye it may look like self-promotion, but trust me it's great business. I apply this approach to even the smallest details to help my company. For example, I use it to get the best media coverage for my company: Since captions for photos identify people left to right, I have become adept at the PR trick of standing to the right of the group facing the camera so my name and my company's name will be listed first.

Although I reflect my company, I can still only be who I am. I do it all honestly. If I didn't, I'd never be able to face myself in the mirror. Honest businesspeople believe in themselves and their companies and never need to hide who they are and what they represent.

I don't and neither should you.

Would I Lie to You?

A while back, I was sitting in a car dealership on the West Coast waiting to finish signing the papers on the new truck my partners and I picked for our business start-up. I was already sold on the truck. I had one exactly like it in Sioux Falls that I liked to drive, and we decided to get the same one there. It might be lousy for parking, but it was great for a six-foot-three-inch guy like me. My partners would use it to haul around the equipment, computers, and servers we used in our business, and I would drive it when I was in town.

Problem was, I wasn't sold on the car salesman. This was my first time meeting him and he seemed nice and affable, but as we swapped stories about sales and business, he seemed a bit off. Still, the deal was fine and I was just there to sign the paperwork so I tried not to get too distracted by my feelings.

But I was.

That's when I spotted a blue Post-it note on his desk, which said in big handwritten letters, "LIE AND FLY." I was not about to ignore that. I read it again to make sure it really said what I thought and then I looked at him. Pointing at the Post-it, I asked, "What's that mean?"

The salesman paused and then leaned across the desk. Maybe he thought I was a kindred spirit from our conversation. Maybe he thought I had already finished signing the papers. Either way, he said, "Okay, I trust you. You get it. It means a lot of times what we do here—not with *you* of course—is 'lie and fly.' The first salesman lies to the customer, telling them what they want to hear and then leaves or flies. Then, a second salesman comes in and works them into the deal we want."

I got it all right. I got that this is not someone I wanted to do business with.

Maybe this guy could look himself in the mirror doing

business this way, but I doubt it. He probably avoided mirrors. And if I let that sale go through, I would violate my principles as a businessman. So, I stood up, shook his hand, thanked him, and walked out. In trying to sell himself, he sold himself and his company right out of a deal, and nobody benefited.

• It's not only about what you're selling; it's about how you're selling it and how you're perceived when you're selling it. That's also why when I say, "Sell you; sell the company" the next four words are: "And do it genuinely."

> **Your Business Has a Personality—Yours**

Companies and their brands have personalities, and those personalities come from its people and you. You are what people see. Selling yourself means selling the business, and this becomes even more important as you move up the proverbial food chain. Just like the physical appearance of a company affects perception of that company, so do its representatives. That's why I cannot be "off" for the brand I am representing: My face needs to be the right face for my business. Jimmy Buffett is a great spokesperson for Margaritaville, but as good a businessman as he is, he would not be much of a spokesman if he owned a Wall Street firm. Speaking of Buffetts, Warren Buffett is not someone you picture hanging with a parrot and drinking a margarita, but millions hang on Warren's every word in corporate America.

In short, you and your people—including your customers—reflect the personality of your company. If you're a bigger business, you want as many of your people as possible out there representing the company. But the positive and (like that car dealership) negative energy in business comes from *you*. We get a sense of a company through its leadership, and the best leaders know they are essential tools in their sales and marketing arsenal. If they excite us, we get excited.

Think about the high-profile big business leaders that you know and admire. Their businesses rise and fall around their leadership for this very reason. Lee Iacocca, Jack Welch, Bob Kraft, Muriel "Mickey" Siebert, Mary Kay Ash, Oprah...Their personalities reflect where their companies are and where they're going. Their names move markets. When Steve Jobs got sick, Apple shares fell as shareholders, employees, and customers reacted.

My experience is that if a leader's relationship to his or her business is honest and direct, what is good for that leader will be good for the company. Actually, I don't know that the two can be separated, at least not anymore. People used to talk about losing your soul when you entered corporate America. But today, as much as a company may want its products and services to speak for it, a business also needs a soul customers can connect with. You need personal connections for more than building relationships in social media—you need them to build and sell the entire company.

But big companies are more in danger than small- and medium-sized businesses of losing that inner soul when they cut jobs. The most recent recession undermined the effectiveness of big businesses to maintain relationships as they tried to make numbers and maintain stock value for their shareholders. Private, small-, and medium-sized businesses, when faced with the same need for cutbacks, can still maintain this personality, largely through staying out there and continuing to deliver on their promises.

I'm not saying this is easy, but I do think it actually can be fun. So get past your fears and get out there and sell yourself. Be the best tool in your toolbox. You know this is about more than selling yourself. Your name might not move markets, but it can still move your marketing in any economy and position you strongly within that market. You can still directly inspire your customers, your employees, and your community as long as you stay who you are. In the small business world if you're well known, well established, and well liked within your community, you can still do business anytime on a handshake. Because you and your business are one and the same—and there is nothing wrong with that.

And in the End...Be Grateful for the Opportunities You Have Had

Early in this book, I told you my three conditions of satisfaction for any work I do: build wealth, grow professionally, and have fun. And succeed or fail, I have taken responsibility for achieving those conditions. I never look for anyone to come running to my aid, but at the same time, I have never been afraid to ask for help—and I will never forget the people who have helped me.

We all had at least one great teacher or someone who helped us along the way. I'll never forget the people who mentored me like John Timmer, Michael O'Connor, and Tom White. I can't forget the people who gave me a chance when I needed it, like Mr. Pinson, who

You Must Give Back

gave me a job in his plumbing company. I was twelve and my dad was serving in Vietnam, and Mr. Pinson hired me so I could earn money, join Big John's Hunting Club, and feel part of the community.

And I am grateful to my family who, in addition to loving me, were also terrific businesspeople. My mom, Henrietta, started as a bookkeeper and became a successful real estate agent, teaching me the importance of doing things exactly right and with great energy. My father, William, repaired B-52 bombers in the Air Force and showed me the importance of organization—of having all the tools you need, making sure those tools are in their proper places, and using them right. And my stepfather, Eugene, owned a number of successful businesses and was always there when I needed some sage advice or to be talked out of a severe case of Johnny Vegas Syndrome.

These people (and many others) helped form my core values and so much of what helps me pass my mirror tests.

• Whether you're looking in the mirror for the first or fiftieth time, ask yourself, *"How will I give back? What will be my legacy?"*

And while you're building that legacy, strive to be thoughtful, considerate, and likable every step of the way—building trust and affinity with everyone you work with and meet, whether they are cleaning your clock or cleaning your house. Think of *everybody* as part of your team. Do this and people will notice.

A few years ago, I was in England in a hotel conference room for an important meeting. Relationships were in the balance; millions of dollars were on the table. And it went brilliantly. We aced the presentation. Right down to the coffee being poured, the production was flawless. So, after the executives said their good-byes and thank-yous, I stayed behind to shake hands and thank the event manager and all the waiters and waitresses too. After all, these are the people who can make and break meet-ings. They control the hospitality while we negotiate our million-dollar deals.

But my PR handler still seemed confused.

"Jeff," he said. "I've never seen anyone do that."

"Do what?" I said.

"Thank the people in the room—the waiters and wait-resses...the help."

"Well, why wouldn't I?"

"No reason," he replied and then paused before con-tinuing. "I guess I just haven't seen anybody do that."

"Wow, really?" I said. "What's the big secret?"

Acknowledgments

To Tami, Lindsey, and Tyler for all they have sacrificed so I can do what I do. To my Mom and Dad for having me and to their spouses and my in-laws for accepting me. To my brothers and sisters for their support.

To Jim, my writer, who adeptly captured my voice and it was just so much fun—you made this easy because you are such a pro. To Rick, my editor, who saw the potential in the proposal and then just said "yes" and "go" and let me be me, and the rest of the team at Hachette, especially Dorothea, Tracy, Rob, and Flag (great cover!). To my agent, Wendy Keller of Keller Media, Inc., who saw the potential in the proposal long before anyone and then would not stop hounding me for fifteen years. And to Julie, Linda, Lisa, and Marlys, the professional executive assistants—they really have run my life and made this possible.

To all of you, thanks!

Appendix

My Business Library "Must" List
(In Alphabetical Order of Authors)

I might love to Tweet and talk, but I also love to read. People who know or follow me will tell you I almost always have a book or three with me on any trip—one of the great pleasures of those long plane rides halfway around the world is I get to read without interruption! As Garrison Keillor said, "A book is a gift you can open again and again." And we may live in a digital world, but books remain essential tools for any businessperson. Books let ideas breathe. They tell great stories. They challenge and inspire you. That's what I hoped to do with *The Mirror Test*. So, as I wrote, I thought about the books in my library by people I admire or that just left a lasting impression on me. This is the list I ended up with. What's on your nightstand?

The Long Tail by Chris Anderson
Barbarians at the Gate: The Fall of RJR Nabisco by
    Bryan Burrough and John Helyar
How to Win Friends & Influence People by Dale Carnegie

Appendix

*Good to Great: Why Some Companies Make the Leap...
and Others Don't* by Jim Collins

The 7 Habits of Highly Effective People by Stephen R.
Covey

The Practice of Management by Peter F. Drucker

The E-Myth by Michael Gerber

*The Tipping Point: How Little Things Can Make a Big
Difference* by Malcolm Gladwell

The Goal: A Process of Ongoing Improvement by Eliyahu
M. Goldratt and Jeff Cox

Think and Grow Rich by Napoleon Hill

Iacocca by Lee Iacocca with William Novak

What Would Google Do? by Jeff Jarvis

Six Pixels of Separation by Mitch Joel

Rich Dad Poor Dad by Robert T. Kiyosaki with Sharon
Lechter

Guerrilla Marketing by Jay Conrad Levinson

*Swim with the Sharks Without Being Eaten Alive: Out-
sell, Outmanage, Outmotivate, and Outnegotiate
Your Competition* by Harvey B. Mackay

The Greatest Salesman in the World by Og Mandino

*In Search of Excellence: Lessons From America's
Best Run Companies* by Thomas J. Peters and Robert
H. Waterman, Jr.

The Wealth of Nations by Adam Smith

Trump: The Art of the Deal by Donald J. Trump with
Tony Schwartz

The Art of War by Sun Tzu

Sam Walton: Made in America by Sam Walton with
John Huey

Secrets of Closing the Sale by Zig Ziglar

Notes

Chapter Six: Adapt or Die

- *Monthly Labor Review* statistics as quoted from Phyllis Korkki, "Hope and Peril After an Escape from the Cubicle," *New York Times*, July 5, 2009, p. 5.

Chapter Eight: The Power of One, Part I

- InfoTrends/CAP Ventures studies quoted from Brent Hoskins, "Variable Data Printing: Boosting Document Value Through Personalization," *Office Technology Magazine* (www.officetechnol ogymag.com), March 2005, p. 10.
- Universal McCann Study: Robert J. Coen, Universal McCann, *Insider's Report*, June 2007.
- As quoted in comScore white paper on catalogs for the United States Postal Service, 2007.
- Direct Marketing Association study as quoted in Levenson et al., pp. 5–6.
- United States Postal Service, "Household Diary Study" as quoted in Levenson et al., p. 6.
- Rochester Institute of Technology study as quoted from Harvey R. Levenson, Ph.D., et al., "The Reality About the Promise of

Printing in the Digital World," Graphic Communication Department California Polytechnic State University, San Luis Obispo, CA, August 2007, p. 6.

Chapter Nine: The Power of One, Part II

- Walt Mossberg and Kara Swisher, "Welcome to Web 3.0," AllTh ingsDigital.com, http://d7.allthingsd.com/20090526/welcome-to -web-30, May 26, 2009.
- Claire Cain Miller, "Spinning the Web: P.R. in Silicon Valley," *New York Times*, July 5, 2009, p. 1.
- Chris Charron, Jaap Favier, and Charlene Li, "Social Computing," Forrester Research, Inc., February 13, 2006, p. 9.

Index

233

Index

Index

Index

Index

Index

Index

Index

240

Index

About the Author

Jeffrey Hayzlett has been called a lot of things, most of them good. He has been described as a "CMO [chief marketing officer] on steroids," who parlayed what he learned running his own businesses into his position as Kodak's CMO, where he helped revitalize one of the world's iconic brands. *Forbes* magazine anointed him the "Celebrity CMO," because of his countless media appearances, including on Donald Trump's *Celebrity Apprentice*. And *Advertising Age* calls him "a new style of CMO," especially for his social media skills that made him one of the top ten C-level executive Twitterers in the world.

Jeff is also a cowboy—literally: He is a South Dakota native who is always wearing cowboy boots and still has a little house on the prairie. When he is not traveling worldwide as a company ambassador and print, social media, and marketing evangelist, he likes nothing more than being on the back of one of his horses out on the range with nothing around for miles. A much sought-after speaker on topics ranging from worldwide business growth, communications, marketing social networking, and mobile marketing, Jeff was named "Marketer of the Year" by *BtoB* magazine in 2008 and has received numerous other marketing and business awards and honors, including the Frost & Sullivan Lifetime Achievement Award for marketing, the prestigious G. D. Crain Jr. Award for excellence from the Business Marketing Association, and the Earl I. Sundeen Award from the International Graphic Arts Education Association for his significant contributions to graphic arts education. He is married to his college sweetheart, Tami, and they have two children, Lindsey and Tyler.

**BUSINESS
PLUS**

Recognized as one of the world's most prestigious business imprints, Business Plus specializes in publishing books that are on the cutting edge. Like you, to be successful we always strive to be ahead of the curve.

Business Plus titles encompass a wide range of books and interests—including important business management works, state-of-the-art personal financial advice, noteworthy narrative accounts, the latest in sales and marketing advice, individualized career guidance, and autobiographies of the key business leaders of our time.

Our philosophy is that business is truly global in every way, and that today's business reader is looking for books that are both entertaining and educational. To find out more about what we're publishing, please check out the Business Plus blog at:

www.businessplusblog.com